The Kingdom of God
And Your Place in the Kingdom

By Jeffery D. Lowe

Copyright © 2008 by Jeffery Lowe

The Kingdom of God
by Jeffery Lowe

Printed in the United States of America

ISBN 978-1-60477-073-5

All rights reserved solely by the author. The author guarantees all contents are original and do not infringe upon the legal rights of any other person or work. No part of this book may be reproduced in any form without the permission of the author. The views expressed in this book are not necessarily those of the publisher.

Unless otherwise indicated, Scripture is taken from the King James Version of the Bible.

Scripture quotations marked "NKJ" are taken from the New King James Version. Copyright © 1979, 1980, 1982 by Thomas Nelson, Inc. Used by permission. All right reserved.

Scripture quotations marked "KW" are taken from The New Testament: An Expanded Translation by Kenneth S. Wuest. Copyright Wm. B. Eerdmans Publishing Co. © 1961. All rights reserved.

www.xulonpress.com

Dedications:

This book is dedicated to all the believers who have been faithful doing the works of Jesus throughout the years. It is also dedicated to God's miracle army of Prophets, Apostles and the believers who will catch the vision and run with it.

Acknowledgements:

For all the inspiration and guidance: Pastor R.D. Sanders, Pastor Daniel Ayettey, Pastors Bayless and Janet Conley, Dr. Chris and Robin Harfouce, and my ever interceding parents; Herman and Karen Lowe.

Table of Contents

Introduction ix

Chapter 1	Kingdom Principles	11
Chapter 2	The Gospel of the Kingdom	15
Chapter 3	The Power of the Kingdom	21
Chapter 4	The Kingdom - God's Dwelling Place on Earth	25
Chapter 5	Who You Are in the Kingdom	29
Chapter 6	The Glory of the Kingdom	37
Chapter 7	The Time of the Kingdom	41
Chapter 8	The Battle of the Kingdom	47
Chapter 9	The Mystery of the Kingdom	61
Chapter 10	The Life of the Kingdom	69
Chapter 11	The Possibilities of the Kingdom	73
Chapter 12	The Finances of the Kingdom	79
Chapter 13	The Angels of the Kingdom	85
Chapter 14	The Judgment of the Kingdom	91
Chapter 15	The Changing of the Kingdom	97
Chapter 16	The Near future of the Kingdom	103
Chapter 17	The Millennium of the Kingdom	107
Chapter 18	Your Place in the Kingdom	117

Introduction

Everyone needs to have a vision. The Holy Spirit is present to accelerate the flame of desire God put in you. To finish the race of life, we must have purpose, vision and understanding. We must be able to see the finish line. We must be able to see: the Kingdom of God.

CHAPTER 1

Kingdom Principles

One of the primary reasons of why Jesus came to the earth was to teach us about the Kingdom of God. Jesus repeatedly preached that the kingdom is at hand [is here]. He preached about the kingdom *more* than being born again (*which was just one time at night, in private*). The destiny of our eternity is just the beginning of our experience with the kingdom. The Kingdom of God is talked about more than seventy times in the New Testament. Jesus also instructed His disciples to preach the same. Even after He rose from the grave, He was seen of His disciples for 40 days and was "...speaking of the things concerning the kingdom of God" (Acts 1:3). Simply put, the kingdom of God is the liberty of spiritual right-standing with God, unceasing joy, and the peace that surpasses all our understanding. In this book, we'll look at some inspirational and interesting life lessons about the kingdom and how we are a vital part of it.

"Then he called his twelve disciples together, and gave them power and authority over all devils, and to cure diseases. And he sent them to preach the kingdom of God, and to heal the sick." Luke 9:1, 2

From the beginning, God said "*Let them have dominion...*" (not "*let us*" have dominion) (Gen 1:26). He set in place a law that He would not change and gave us permanent legal authority on Earth. God dominated the invisible world, but we have title to the visible. We are here to colonize Earth with heaven and establish it as a territory of the invisible world. If anything happens or does not happen, it is in man's hands. When we rule it with the power and authority that God has given us, the will of the Father will be done on earth as it is in heaven. Jesus came to show us the authority we have. The connection with the Holy Spirit *"will guide you into all truth..."* and teaches us all things; and is vital for our continuous life instruction (John 16:13).

"... What is man that You are mindful of him, Or the son of man that You take care of him? You have made him a little lower than the angels; You have crowned him with glory and honor, And set him over the works of Your hands. You have put all things in subjection under his feet." For in that He put all in subjection under him, He left nothing that is not put under him. But now we do not yet see all things put under him. " Hebrews 2:6-8 (NKJ)

"The heaven, even the heavens, are the LORD's: but the earth hath he given to the children of men." Psalm 115:16

"Verily I say unto you, Whatsoever ye shall bind on earth shall be bound in heaven: and whatsoever ye shall loose on earth shall be loosed in heaven." Matthew 18:18

The bible mentions two people who are called the son of God: Jesus, and also Adam in Luke 3:38. When Adam let go of his original authority, he not only lost a father, but a kingdom. He gave it to Satan, who now uses beasts of the earth against us. Even the plants are used against us (*tobacco, marijuana, cocaine and the fermentation to make alcoholic drinks*). We should dominate the plants, not have the plants dominate us. The Lord left man a promise that a

Messiah King would redeem man, restore and re-establish the kingdom with sons, instead of servants.

"Wherefore, as by one man sin entered into the world, and death by sin; and so death passed upon all men, for that all have sinned" Romans 5:12

"But as many as received him, to them gave he power to become the sons of God, even to them that believe on his name" John 1:12

"...Verily, verily, I say unto you, Whosoever committeth sin is the servant of sin. And the servant abideth not in the house for ever: but the Son abideth ever." John 8:34, 35

We have a natural instinct to control our circumstances and environment. It is not for dominating other people, as witches and spiritism attempt to do; but is our original power through the government of God. Man is God's legal agency and access through earth. We grant Him permission with prayer. God can do anything (except change or go back on His word), but we have the license on the earth to allow what happens in the seen world. The earth is the Lords' and the meek shall inherit it as sons.

The world system is designed by the devil to make us fail. He had us put on a covering or "coat" of sin nature. The Word gave us a way to escape and has completed His side of our covenant agreement. The rest is up to us. The amount of effort we put into our "fight of faith" will determine our success in using what is available in Christ. Even when we have received a new nature, our old way of thinking is used to put that old weighty coat, or "old man" back on us. It takes time for us to renew our mind to get in agreement with our born again spirit.

"Lie not one to another, seeing that ye have put off the old man with his deeds; And have put on the new man, which is renewed in knowledge after the image of him that created him" Colossians 3:9,10

The enemy has been defeated long ago, but his words and doctrines may still exist in the battle fields of many minds. Some of us who have been in the world for so long that we obtain a prodigal son's mentality, desiring to be like a hired servant instead of a son (the Father's desire). Some have had the mental slavery, or hopelessness, similar to the children of Egypt who wanted to go back and be slaves instead of conquerors (Num 14:4). Some have been satisfied with becoming dependents instead of disciples; or children instead of sons. Some buy into the false reality of fantasies with the opposite sex; or have hate, envy, covetousness for another, or other ways of that are not kingdom thinking. We learn about God's kingdom to understand the true reality of who we are and what we have; to live more abundantly ourselves and to free the slaves of the world system.

"...If ye continue in my word, then are ye my disciples indeed; and ye shall know the truth, and the truth shall make you free." John 8:31, 32

CHAPTER 2

The Gospel of the Kingdom

The gospel is a spiritual way of life in the kingdom of God; a life that answers the yearning in our God-given spirit.

"The law and the prophets were until John: since that time the kingdom of God is preached, and every man presseth into it." Luke 16:16.

The gospel, or good news, has dominion over unfavorable circumstances. Jesus preached deliverance with a dominion over poverty, sickness, death, and any and all types of bondage; including the fear of physical or spiritual death.

"And deliver them who through fear of death were all their lifetime subject to bondage." Hebrews 2:15.

For centuries upon centuries, many of us have had a watered down message teaching only "religion" or only helping out in the natural, which could only take us so far. But many in this world would be quick to embrace the kingdom message and denounce any "religion" that the world has to offer, because the kingdom is not a religion, but a government of heavenly relationship with our Father.

"For unto us a child is born, unto us a son is given: and the government shall be upon his shoulder: and his

name shall be called Wonderful, Counsellor, The mighty God, The everlasting Father, The Prince of Peace. Of the increase of his government and peace there shall be no end, upon the throne of David, and upon his kingdom, to order it, and to establish it..." Isaiah 9:6, 7**

Jesus went teaching the gospel of the kingdom. **"And Jesus went about all Galilee, teaching in their synagogues, and preaching the gospel of the kingdom, and healing all manner of sickness and all manner of disease among the people." Matthew 4:23** He taught His disciples to do the same. **"And as ye go, preach, saying, The kingdom of heaven is at hand..." Matt 10:7 "And heal the sick that are therein, and say unto them, The kingdom of God is come nigh unto you." Luke 10:9.** He told them to preach efficiently, not about the miracles He did, but about His **kingdom**. When they preached the **kingdom**, the miracles followed them. **"And the seventy returned again with joy, saying, Lord, even the devils are subject unto us through thy name." Luke 10:19** The apostle Paul followed in his footsteps. **"And he went into the synagogue and spake boldly for the space of three months, disputing and persuading the things concerning the kingdom of God." Acts 19:8**

A lot of messages from ministers, missionaries and pastors will stop at the cross, the blood, or the resurrection, but won't touch the desires of our earthly life that we yearn for in our earthly life. These messages were important to give us birth, but Jesus came to give us a life more abundant than just existing. *"If we live in the Spirit, let us also walk in the Spirit."* (Galatians 5:25).

Jesus said a kingdom is like a man who went into a far country to receive himself a kingdom, and to return. He told His servants, "...*occupy until I come*" (Luke 19:12, 13). The bride of Christ will *"make herself* ready" until *"the king-*

doms of this world have become the kingdoms of our Lord" (Revelation 19:7; 11:15).

Jesus is not coming back until the mandate in Matthew 24:14 is fulfilled.

"And this gospel of the kingdom shall be preached in all the world for a witness unto all nations; and then shall the end come."

As a whole, the Church itself has barely gotten the message and has much division. Some think the gospel is just a message about the death, burial, and resurrection; leaving total salvation incomplete (*If you are saved, what are you saved from?*). If you took a show of hands in almost any church, most in the congregations have needs for healing, finances, or other miracles that are commonplace in kingdom living. That should be the response when we go *outside of the church*. Until we preach what Jesus said to preach, the end will not come. We should preach *the same as He did*, not just preach of the things He did.

You cannot have faith in what you don't know or what you hear very little. Faith has to be bigger than what you're experiencing or it is not faith. You cannot live beyond your own belief. If you don't believe for more than what your parents had, or have taught you, you will receive the religion that your parents have received; and the same problems, diseases. And, you could die like they did if there is a limit on how far your faith goes. You will live off the revelation you have. You will either think like God, or think like men.

Your faith determines your life; "*...according to your faith be it unto you*" (Matthew 9:29). When you become more confident that "*...the kingdom of God is within you*" (Luke 17:21), you will preach this gospel of the kingdom and the signs will follow you as a believer.

"And he said unto them, Go ye into all the world, and preach the gospel to every creature." Mark 16:15

"And these signs shall follow them that believe; In my name shall they cast out devils; they shall speak with new tongues; They shall take up serpents; and if they drink any deadly thing, it shall not hurt them; they shall lay hands on the sick, and they shall recover." Mark 16:17, 18.

With faith, you will learn, expect, and experience all the life and promises that God has taught us from the beginning. When Satan came to prove, or "tempt" Jesus in the wilderness, he quoted word from the Old Testament about living from every word (*rhema*) from God, worshipping God, and divine protection. Jesus proved that kingdom living had come down to the earth and the devil has begged, trembled, and ran ever since, from those who received the authority of their kingship and rule on this planet. Satan had heard about, but had not seen this kind of resistance since before the fall of Adam. Listen to your faith which is inside you. Your faith is not impressed with your limitations, but only the power of the gospel.

Jesus is called "King of kings", not king of servants (1Timothy 6:15). To those who have accepted a relationship with the main message and purpose of Jesus are no longer servants.

"No longer do I call you servants, for a servant does not know what his master is doing; but I have called you friends, for all things that I heard from My Father I have made known to you." John 15:15 (NKJ)

In our friendship he continues to reveal more to us.

"...it is given unto you to know the mysteries of the kingdom of heaven, but to them it is not given. For whosoever hath, to him shall be given, and he shall have more abundance: but whosoever hath not, from him shall be taken away even that he hath" Matthew 13:11, 12.

In the U.S. we have many converts, but not enough disciples. Sometimes 'religion' will steal them away since they can't make them. If you follow what you understand in the natural, you will have what you see. If you can *perceive* the boundless potential in the spiritual, you will *receive* what you believe. In the natural you look at common circumstances, popular opinion, and experiences and think - like the world does - that Jesus died and, at best, retired. But in the spiritual, you believe that we serve a living God. You know these are still the bible days. God's Word is His bond and we can take the Word at face value. We are more than conquerors. Even as Jesus is, so are we in the world. We will do greater works. We will live and not die. The Spirit of God will be upon us to defeat every temporary circumstance the devil put in motion. Jesus is doing even more now than He did when He walked on the earth.

"But rather seek ye the kingdom of God; and all these things shall be added unto you. Fear not, little flock; for it is your Father's good pleasure to give you the kingdom." Luke12:31, 32

CHAPTER 3

The Power of the Kingdom

If you want more faith, then study, read and listen to the Word. If you want more power, keep in prayer; giving a constant ear to the Spirit. Our Father God has delivered us from the power of darkness and has translated us into the Kingdom of his Son. Because we are made fit to be partakers of the inheritance of the saints in light, Jesus gave us power to become sons of God.

"Giving thanks unto the Father, which hath made us meet to be partakers of the inheritance of the saints in light: who hath delivered us from the power of darkness, and hath translated us into the kingdom of his dear Son" Colossians 1:13

In these days it is challenging to preach without power. Some of God's people suffer because they choose not to use the power they have been given (Hosea 4:6). We have been given power to be an effective witness; so that we won't just have a promise, but *an experience.*

"But ye shall receive power, after that the Holy Ghost is come upon you: and ye shall be witnesses unto me…" Acts 1:8

The illumination we have is knowledge of the availability of God and the acceleration of His kingdom, on earth as it is in heaven, with an ability that is far above our own. First Corinthians 4:20 says, *"For the Kingdom of God is not in word, but in power."*

Two Greek words for power; |exousia (authority) and dunamis (high power, Spirit of God himself) became the difference between the delegated authority of the disciples and to the accelerated activity of the Holy Spirit which leads us to press into God's kingdom and gathers the spoils of His victory, giving back to the 'body' of Christ what was always rightfully ours.

John taught the character of God (serving and loving your neighbor). Jesus taught the power of God (the gospel of the kingdom). Some ministries are still limited to John's ministry, denying the power of God.

"This know also, that in the last days perilous times shall come. For men shall be lovers of their own selves, covetous, boasters, proud, blasphemers, disobedient to parents, unthankful, unholy…highminded, lovers of pleasures more than lovers of God; Having a form of godliness, but denying the power thereof: from such turn away." 2 Timothy 3:1-5

The people who don't gather the spoils of the enemy from the victory of the Lamb will actually scatter (Greek – "scorpizo"- representing a scorpion or enemy) people away by representing a portion of God and a portion of the opinion of the adversary.

"But if I with the finger of God cast out devils, no doubt the kingdom of God is come upon you. When a strong man armed keepeth his palace, his goods are in peace: But when a stronger than he shall come upon him, and overcome him, he taketh from him all his armour wherein he trusted, and divideth his spoils. He that is not with me is against me: and he that gathereth not with me scattereth." Luke 11:21, 22

This is being unfruitful is being unstable in all ways, double-minded, and trying to serve two masters.

John 3:3 says, being born again is being able to "*see the kingdom of God.*" It is to obtain the righteousness, or right-standing, of God Himself; someone who is *called*. Someone who is holy, or set apart from the world, will have an abundance of the Kingdom of our Lord ministered unto him; someone that is *sent*. God will first give you the desire and then the ability to perform with His Word.

"For he who lacks these things is shortsighted, even to blindness, and has forgotten that he was cleansed from his old sins. Therefore, brethren, be even more diligent to make your call and election sure, for if you do these things you will never stumble; for so an entrance will be supplied to you abundantly into the everlasting kingdom of our Lord and Savior Jesus Christ." 2 Peter 1:9-11 (NKJ)

The later will be greater than the former. The anointing for which the past generation of saints have been praying and fasting is now here. The same word that says you can be saved if you believe, says, "*...all things are possible to him who believeth*" (Mark 9:23).

What does this mean? It means the unlimited, residential power of God which evidences the resurrected Christ in us, and that could move sycamore trees, mountains, strongholds, and even control climates - is in you. It means the power to clear out hospitals and morgues. It means the spirit of infirmities, cancer, heart conditions, asthma, AIDS, and all the curses from the enemy have to bow down and answer to the power of the Holy Spirit in you. It means listening to the voice of the Spirit when He says, "*Can these bones live?*" And *you* prophecy to the bones as you are commanded and watch as bone connects to bone and sinews; and flesh comes upon them; and breath on the slain so they may live as in the 37th chapter of Ezekiel.

"Marvel not at this: for the hour is coming, in the which all that are in the graves shall hear his voice" John 5:28

We were once far off from God in the Old Testament days. But the days of God just being in the cloud, the burning bush, or the tent, are over. God is now in us to the point that His words *abide in us*.

"If you abide in Me, and My words abide in you, you will ask what you desire, and it shall be done for you. By this My Father is glorified, that you bear much fruit; so you will be My disciples...These things I have spoken to you, that My joy may remain in you, and that your joy may be full." John 15:7, 8, 11 (NKJ)

Full joy comes from divine health, salvation for family members, perfect peace, calling things that are not as though they are, and knowing you have all power over the enemy. We have more power then we can use in our lifetime. Our Spirit inspired words carry a lot of power. They go into bones and mend them. They talk to eyes so they can see; they talk to ears so they can hear. We are clothed with the antidote for any sickness or disease. This is the **power** of the kingdom of God.

"Herein is our love made perfect, that we may have boldness in the day of judgment: because as he is (Jesus), so are we in this world." 1 John 4:17

When you see into the realm of the Spirit, you take your eyes off the world of temporary circumstances and look into the future with God; and He will show you things to come.

"However, when He, the Spirit of truth, has come, He will guide you into all truth; for He will not speak on His own authority, but whatever He hears He will speak; and He will tell you things to come." John 16:13 (NKJ)

CHAPTER 4

The Kingdom - God's Dwelling Place on Earth

God has given us the planet. We were created to have dominion.

"You have made him to have dominion over the works of Your hands; You have put all things under his feet" Psalm 8:6 (NKJ)

Instructions from heaven were given (*let your will be done on earth as it is in heaven*) for *us* to 'replenish' the earth with heavenly dominion and power. Adam, the original "governor" of the planet had failed to accomplish this responsibility. But, The Son of God was *given* to us as promised. We would return to a dominion of a kingdom that would be set up and have no end.

"I saw in the night visions, and, behold, one like the Son of man came with the clouds of heaven, and came to the Ancient of days, and they brought him near before him. And there was given him dominion, and glory, and a kingdom...his dominion is an everlasting dominion, which shall not pass away, and his kingdom that which shall not be destroyed." Dan 7:13, 14

All the things Jesus fought for and won has been given to his saints that they would not lack.

"...having wiped out the handwriting of requirements that was against us, which was contrary to us. And He has taken it out of the way, having nailed it to the cross. Having disarmed principalities and powers, He made a public spectacle of them, triumphing over them in it." Col 2:14, 15

We now represent Him in word and deed.

"...ye are enriched by him, in all utterance, and in all knowledge; Even as the testimony of Christ was confirmed in you: So that ye come behind in no gift..." 1 Corinthians 1:5-7

His victory put us back in right standing with God, so we have no reason to settle for mediocrity. We should desire the best gifts, since they are available.

"But earnestly desire the best gifts. And yet I show you a more excellent way" 1 Corinthians 1:12:31

When the promise becomes a corporate life experience in the unity of the body of Christ, the greatness of the everlasting kingdom will be fully known; the body of Christ, the Word of God. Every knee should bow, now.

"And the kingdom and dominion, and the greatness of the kingdom under the whole heaven, shall be given to the people of the saints of the most High, whose kingdom is an everlasting kingdom, and all dominions shall serve and obey him." Daniel 7:27

People had waited for the kingdom of God in the time of Jesus.

"And, behold, there was a man named Joseph, a counsellor; and he was a good man, and a just... he was of Arimathaea, a city of the Jews: who also himself waited for the kingdom of God." Luke 23:50, 51

Many self-righteous Jewish leaders, having a desire for their own dominion and the influence of money and people, rejected the kingdom of God, thinking that they could own it with their own power were rebuked by Jesus.

"Therefore I say to you, the kingdom of God will be taken from you and given to a nation bearing the fruits of it" Matthew 21:43

When the disciples thought the kingdom of God would immediately appear, Jesus told them the parable about a certain nobleman who went into a far country to receive himself a kingdom (*parable of talents*; Luke 19:11-27) saying "occupy, until I come", and another about a husbandman who went into a far country for a long time (Luke 20:9-18), sending a servant and finally his own Son, to reap the fruit of his vineyard. In the same way, men were placed here to rule with His spirit of love upon the earth with the Father's influence, so He could come for His harvest.

"Therefore be patient, brethren, until the coming of the Lord. See how the farmer waits for the precious fruit of the earth, waiting patiently for it until it receives the early and latter rain." James 5:7 (NKJ)

The angel Lucifer was cast out of heaven for his ambitions. He did not want to serve the heirs of God, but wanted his throne above all. He beguiled Eve with the false promise of power, to temporarily take dominion over God's colony. But now that Jesus has taken *"captivity captive and given gifts unto men,"* (Ephesians 4:8), He tells us to obey His commandments and teach men to do so (Matthew 28:20).

The commandments from Moses were not life giving, but Jesus abundantly reminded us of the authority we've had since the beginning of time, putting on a spiritual show and tell, delivering us from the power of darkness, into the kingdom of His dear son.

For every temptation, device, sickness, disease or even death, there's a way to escape into God's dwelling place, the kingdom of God. Those who know and desire the spiritual will have the influence of the Governor, ruling with Him in heavenly places. They will leave an open door for the Holy Spirit to come upon them receiving the favor and prosperity of God, to replenish the earth for a harvest the world has never seen.

CHAPTER 5

Who You Are in the Kingdom

God has validated you. Not for any works you've done, race or gender, but because of your response to His Word of love.

"But as many as received him, to them gave he power to become the sons of God, even to them that believe on his name" John 1:12

He is praying for you that your faith never fails. He identifies us as His children and joint-heirs with Christ (Romans 8:17). His desire is to give you His glory and be one with Him.

"I do not pray for these alone, but also for those who will believe in Me through their word; that they all may be one, as You, Father, *are* in Me, and I in You; that they also may be one in Us, that the world may believe that You sent Me. And the glory which You gave Me I have given them, that they may be one just as We are one" John 17:20-22 (NKJ)

He has made you more than just a conqueror and has written your name in heaven as royalty.

"And hath raised us up together, and made us sit together in heavenly places in Christ Jesus" Ephesians 2:6

"And hath made us kings and priests unto God and his Father; to him be glory and dominion for ever and ever. Amen." Revelation 1:6

"But you *are* a chosen generation, a royal priesthood, a holy nation, His own special people, that you may proclaim the praises of Him who called you out of darkness into His marvelous light" 1 Peter 2:9 (NKJ)

He wants you to provide proof that His love and power is alive and well.

"But you shall receive power when the Holy Spirit has come upon you; and you shall be witnesses to Me in Jerusalem, and in all Judea and Samaria, and to the end of the earth." Acts 1:8

If any man be in Christ, "*he is a new creature...*" (2 Corinthians 5:17). Since salvation is just the beginning of our experience with God, we must search the scriptures to learn what He has called us to be. Since God knows the power that He put in us, He knows the potential His 'Seed' will specifically produce in you. He knows when you develop a true hunger for the Word, He will place mentors around you, as you look for people that share your vision for the high calling of God, and eliminate Spirit quenching, growth stunting, faithless "I'll believe-it-when-I-see-it" people that want to sit on the 'front row' in the theater of your life. He is more than willing to send you, and to provide the words and foresight you need to accomplish salvation and discipleship to your friends, family and circle of influence. When you know the availability of grace to get rid of sin is possible with Him, you will learn that you don't have to try so hard to do right, but just follow the ever-present leading of the Spirit.

Satan has put up a fight in the minds of the uninformed. Years after the resurrection, he tried to convince many that God didn't 'so love the world' or that you had to work for your salvation, as if the blood of Jesus only made a down payment for your sins. When Martin Luther and others spread

The Kingdom of God

the word after the 16th century, he still tried to convince others that God wasn't a healing God and miracles died with Jesus. Now that many more people are getting saved and healed these days more than any other time in history, he still tries to stall for time with distractions of the world, or telling us God's word doesn't apply today. His biggest function is to try to convince you that your heavenly identity is not what God's word says it is. As soon as the church recognizes that as a whole, he's finished. People even now (*whether in or out the church*) are recognizing the imposters or backsliding leaders in the church who have not been called by God, but have called themselves, or are there to please people and not God.

Your identity is in who God says you are - a son or a daughter. Not a wretch, but royalty. You are not trying to "let your little light shine" but you are the light of the world even as He is the light of the world. You are not trying to spend your days trying to get to heaven, but letting God's will be done on earth as it is in heaven. Your righteous prayers are always heard by the Father. If a legion of demons knew Jesus answers prayer, surely we know God will answer the request of His children.

"So the demons begged Him, saying, "If You cast us out, permit us to go away into the herd of swine." And He said to them, "Go"... " Matthew 8:31, 32 (NKJ)

He calls us doers of the word by our intentions, before we have done anything. He does not look on your past where you have sinned, but your future. The blood of Jesus has justified you into right standing with God. You are not a sinner saved by grace, but called to grace to lead others to the Light of the world (*the bible calls saved people "saints" 330 times; unsaved people "sinners" 240 times; and saved people "sinners" 0 times*)

We grow up as children of God, and then becoming sons as we mature in the faith.

"Now I say, That the heir, as long as he is a child, differeth nothing from a servant, though he be lord of all But is under tutors and governors until the time appointed of the father." Galatians 4:1, 2

Jesus has called us to "*present our bodies a living sacrifice...*" (Romans 12:1). He wouldn't ask us to do anything He would not do himself. When we deny our selfish way of thinking, or self rule, we began a life fulfilling journey to bring reconciliation of God with men.

When God calls us out of darkness, we need to continue to renew our mind away from any prison of condemnation that the adversary tries to retain us in. The truth will only make you free if you know it.

You will not be like the world where seeing is believing. But, rather like unto a son of God, where believing is seeing. This is the kind of faith that is pleasing to God. It is in a place in the spiritual realm of God where you can see your identification or "badge" of authority. It is the place where you exercise your rights you've been given. If a person is faithful in the area that they have been given, God will promote them and increase their level of responsibility.

"His lord said to him, 'Well *done,* good and faithful servant; you have been faithful over a few things, I will make you ruler over many things. Enter into the joy of your lord." Matthew 25:23 (NKJ)

"He that is faithful in that which is least is faithful also in much..." Luke 16:10

Start off with the little faith you have for the small things (*i.e. headaches, sniffles, a peaceful day*) and build up your faith by consistently hearing about your power for the bigger things (*i.e. cursing tumors, raising the dead*). When you are faithful over little He will make you faithful over much. You are anointed to overcome every affliction, addiction and curse upon the Earth. Begin where you have confidence and build yourself in the faith. When you are praying for another person, give them words of faith so they can be in agreement with you. Allow the Holy Spirit to guide you as each person and situation is different, since there is no "cookie-cutter" formula. The different blind people that Jesus healed had different levels of faith and either got an immediate miracle or a delayed one. Sometimes, the Lord would just touch someone without a word spoken (Matthew 8:15). The Holy Spirit has used me in many different ways with His power, even as He will use you to do greater works. You can find promises in God's Word for any need.

You are called to be the walking revelation of the power of Jesus Christ. He has approved you to represent heaven on earth. His Word must become so real to you that you can immediately detect and reject a word that does not come from God.

"Casting down imaginations, and every high thing that exalteth itself against the knowledge of God, and bringing into captivity every thought to the obedience of Christ" 2 Corinthians 10:5

Use the bible as a mirror for your life to see your true self in it. It tells you who God said you are and what you should do. You must learn what God is responsible for and what you are responsible to do. It is written for believers. Believers who will have faith and act on what they know. You must decide you are the one who believes it over every other report. Refuse to be moved by what you see or feel. Put off your 'old-man' or worldly way of thinking and put on the armour of God.

"...put off concerning the former conversation the old man, which is corrupt according to the deceitful lusts; and be renewed in the spirit of your mind; and that ye put on the new man, which after God is created in righteousness and true holiness." Ephesians 4:22-25

Once you know the will of God, nobody will be able to talk you out of it. The devil can't take advantage of someone who knows how to hold onto the Word of God 24/7. We are here to remind the devil that he's a failure.

We have rightfully been given authority, but we can choose whether to use this or not. We have liberty to exercise His dominion, and the privilege to enforce His word, operating in full capacity. The purpose of this authority is to make all the resources of God accessible to the believer. Great power in God is not far off and out of reach for the chosen, *you* are the chosen. Great power brings results to the battlefield. There is no limit to your jurisdiction. It goes beyond the highest stars and below the deepest sea. Tumors have to dissolve when we speak to them. Diseases have to stop when we give the Word. You have a blank check for the power of God. The only limit is your faith. The level of power in your life is directly proportional to how you talk, what you think about, who you spend your time with, and how you spend your days.

It is not only what you believe that helps you; it's what you do with what you know.

"You believe that there is one God. You do well. Even the demons believe—and tremble!" James 2:19 (NKJ)

Your faith will speak to you and tell on you, especially when the storms of life come. You should not have more than enough of the power of God you'll ever need and seldom turn on the "switch". Faith comes by hearing, but works come by doing. Listen to the faith that's within you that's always in touch with the Holy Spirit.

When you are convinced of the reality of God, you will dismiss lying symptoms, situations and imaginations. You will enforce your rule with the power of His name. The Word is not bound for you to correct any situation and eject any adversary in your way. When you know you are sent by God, you know you have the authority over death, hell and the grave. The saints that speak His report will see heaven validate their words. The testimony of the Word is also the spirit of prophecy (Revelation 19:10). You can foresee your

The Kingdom of God

[Handwritten annotations: "Prayer sees what already available" / "Promise of God is the title deed" / "Our faith completes the transaction of the word"]

victory, and the victory coming for others. Those who are well trained in the Word will win every battle.

You are a danger to the devil when you know the will of God and that you're in His perfect will. You know who you are and what you are called to do. You are fearless and authoritative. You are not in the process of trying things, but you know things. You have the Spirit to give you the 'how to'. You don't come boldly to the throne and beg, or wonder around, you know the blood gave you the right not to just hope for the best, but expect it. The devil doesn't devour you, he flees from you. Don't settle for anything less than His divine will. Pursue what belongs to you!

"Therefore submit to God. Resist the devil and he will flee from you. Draw near to God and He will draw near to you. Cleanse *your* hands, *you* sinners; and purify *your* hearts, *you* double-minded." James 4:7, 8 (NKJ)

You must have faith to understand the Word of God. The Word is not an opinion, but a person. You cannot put it 'on a shelf' with stories from the 5:00 news. The same Word that guarantees forgiveness of sins is the same Word that guarantees healing from sickness and disease. We are not healed when we receive, but healed when we *believe*. We are not saved when we 'get there', but saved when we believe. Our faith completes our transaction and makes us whole and lacking nothing. The promise of God is the title deed to what is rightfully yours by the divine blood of Jesus.

The Word of God or 'seed' in our life must have the spiritual nutrients to produce a harvest. It must be in a good climate with plenty of illumination so that His victory is our victory. It must be on good ground to bear the fruit for the nations. The Seed must continue in the Word by continued hearing and prayer.

Prayer enables or reminds the believer to see what is already available. Not the long labored "begging God to do something" prayers, but a lifestyle of prayer and peace. As prayer positions and revives our soul, it also tunes us into the throne room of God. When you go that place that surpasses knowledge, the knowledge becomes experience.

"And to know the love of Christ, which passeth knowledge, that ye might be filled with all the fulness of God." Ephesians 3:19

This is a place where revelation not only generates expectation, but obtains the experience of the promise with performance. It is then when we see the fruits of what we are called to do, and people will know of a truth, that we are proof providers of a risen and living Savior.

CHAPTER 6

The Glory of the Kingdom

We are born to carry the presence of God. He has called you into His kingdom and glory. Jesus included us all in His prayer.

"I do not pray for these alone, but also for those who will believe in Me through their word; that they all may be one, as You, Father, *are* in Me, and I in You; that they also may be one in Us, that the world may believe that You sent Me. And the glory which You gave Me I have given them, that they may be one just as We are one" **John 17:20-22 (NKJ)**

The resident power of God in us, is here to give the evidence of a resurrected, living Christ.

"And as ye go, preach, saying, The kingdom of heaven is at hand. Heal the sick, cleanse the lepers, raise the dead, cast out devils: freely ye have received, freely give." **Matthew 10:7, 8**

We are here to be proof providers that He lives, has all power, and has intentionally passed this to us to glorify God. When we willingly submit to God, He justifies us and allows His glory in us to reflect the His glory to others.

"For whom he did foreknow, he also did predestinate to be conformed to the image of his Son, that he might be the firstborn among many brethren. Moreover whom he did predestinate, them he also called: and whom he called, them he also justified: and whom he justified, them he also glorified." **Romans 8:29, 30**

In the *past*, we *have* sinned and come short of the glory of God, but now, we are changing into the image of Christ, the Spirit of God with the glory of God abiding in us, going back to God's original plan, to be made in His image and likeness.

"But we all, with open face beholding as in a glass the glory of the Lord, are changed into the same image from glory to glory, even as by the Spirit of the LORD." 2 Corinthians 3:18

Our born again spirit, that is always in tune with God more than our minds (hearts), is being nourished with God's living word by the Holy Spirit, to accelerate into the glory of God into a state of knowing, that's beyond all natural comprehension.

When Peter, James and John saw Moses and Elijah in **glory** (Matthew 17:1-3), they knew who they were without seeing any pictures of them, like the 'rich man' seen Abraham (Luke 16:23), but was in a state of mind not limited with the bodies we have now. Isaiah and John also interpreted the voices of holy angels in their own language (see Isaiah 6:3, Revelation 4:8). With the glory in us, men of God have so much potential for deep perception with the word of knowledge and wisdom, as in Paul's case, the perception to see the need for repentance and healing.

"Repent therefore of this thy wickedness, and pray God, if perhaps the thought of thine heart may be forgiven thee. For I perceive that thou art in the gall of bitterness, and in the bond of iniquity." Acts 8:22, 23

"The same heard Paul speak: who stedfastly beholding him, and perceiving that he had faith to be healed, said

with a loud voice, Stand upright on thy feet. And he leaped and walked." Acts 14:9, 10

Because the Spirit knows all things and gives us insight, we can use the glory in us for kingdom purposes.

"And thus are the secrets of his heart made manifest; and so falling down on his face he will worship God, and report that God is in you of a truth." 1 Corinthians 14:25

With the glory of the kingdom you have the ability not only to talk about what's coming, but to *deliver what is already available*. Our **glorified** spirit is given instructions to use the power and authority within us that's greater than whoever is in the world. The Word already had victory in heaven, but a Son was given to lead us to a change of nature to change the Earth. We neglect our second nature and hold onto our first.

"**Therefore if any man be in Christ, he is a new creature: old things are passed away; behold, all things are become new.**" 2 Corinthians 5:17

God is looking for a person who He can show himself mightily. When you stop thinking about *what you are going to do* and start thinking what God is going to do, you've just stepped into a higher realm of God. Listen to His promptings, and His insight and favor will take you to a higher level than you've expected Him to take you. It is a great thing to receive the promise, but the greatest miracle is holding on to it. In time, your consistency will make it easier to perform miracles than to give alms to a beggar. It will become easier to heal with your shadow or handkerchief than to tell someone "just wait on the lord" or God will do it "in his own time". Any disease on the planet will have to bow down from the glorious presence of God in us. We have now begun to realize the King of Glory has left us in control with His authority and power to have *kingdom glory and dominion*.

"Grace and peace be multiplied unto you through the knowledge of God, and of Jesus our Lord, According as his divine power hath given unto us all things that pertain unto life and godliness, through the knowledge of him that hath called us to glory and virtue: Whereby are given unto us exceeding great and precious promises: that by these ye might be partakers of the divine nature, having escaped the corruption that is in the world through lust."
2 Peter 1:2-4

We don't have to look at ourselves as having an inferior power than Jesus, because we are also sons with the power of God in us to do greater. We realize that His power has given us <u>all</u> things that pertain to life and godliness, because we are called to glory and virtue. Prepare to express the glory of the kingdom that Jesus has given you, unto the world.

CHAPTER 7

The Time of the Kingdom

Man was not created to dwell in time. He was created with dominion over it. When the devil fell from immortality to mortality, he set his mind on man to bring them into his temporal world, dwelling in a place of darkness away from the illuminating understanding of the Word of God.

"...Woe to the inhabiters of the earth and of the sea! for the devil is come down unto you, having great wrath, because he knoweth that he hath but a short time." Revelation 12:12

When sin entered into the world, mankind fell into the essence of time, and we no longer had dominion over time or life. After that sixth day, the works of God creation ceased from the earth.

"Wherefore, as by one man sin entered into the world, and death by sin; and so death passed upon all men... Nevertheless death reigned from Adam to Moses, even over them that had not sinned after the similitude of Adam's transgression, who is the figure of him that was to come." Romans 5:12

What became a downfall in the beginning is now our most valuable asset. Time increases faith and provides growth. God made 'days' so we could redeem and manage time, to replenish the earth; and the light of joy to rule over the sadness in darkness. He placed a great light (the sun) in the sky for a physical representation of the Sun of righteousness, the Son of God.

"And God made two great lights; the greater light to rule the day, and the lesser light to rule the night: he made the stars also. And God set them in the firmament of the heaven to give light upon the earth, And to rule over the day and over the night, and to divide the light from the darkness: and God saw that it was good." **Genesis 1:16-18**

"But unto you that fear my name shall the Sun of righteousness arise with healing in his wings; and ye shall go forth, and grow up as calves of the stall." **Malachi 4:2**

God manifested Himself as Alpha and Omega, the image of God, in time, in the flesh, to destroy the works of the devil (Colossians 1:15).

"And without controversy great is the mystery of godliness: God was manifest in the flesh, justified in the Spirit, seen of angels, preached unto the Gentiles, believed on in the world, received up into glory." **1 Timothy 3:16**

"...the devil sinneth from the beginning. For this purpose the Son of God was manifested, that he might destroy the works of the devil." **1 John 3:8**

The Lord sits at the right hand of God until the fullness of times until all things are gathered together.

"The LORD said unto my Lord, Sit thou at my right hand, until I make thine enemies thy footstool." **Psalm 110:1**

"Having made known unto us the mystery of his will, according to his good pleasure which he hath purposed in himself: That in the dispensation of the fulness of times he might gather together in one all things in Christ, both which are in heaven, and which are on earth; even in him" Ephesians 1:9, 10

And now he sits at the right hand of God until the times when all is restored.

"And he shall send Jesus Christ, which before was preached unto you: Whom the heaven must receive until the times of restitution of all things, which God hath spoken by the mouth of all his holy prophets since the world began." Acts 3:20, 21

We, who have received (*dunamis*) power to become sons of God, will also have Satan under our feet with the resident power of God in us, who knew us before the beginning of time.

Time gives us an experience, a beginning and a closure of all that we fell into. All these times have a purpose under heaven. Each one of our times for birth has been carefully and intelligently chosen by God. We are handpicked to live in these last days. After eternity is permanently placed in our hearts, God will wipe away every tear and the former shall not be remembered, or come to mind because there is no place for them in an eternal, abundant life.

Our Father in heaven sees all time at once, not unlike when we see all the numbers on a clock at the same time. Is, (*or existing*) is the only tense in the presence of the Father. The 'was', or the 'will be', is represented from heaven as the Alpha & Omega. Even after we have stopped praying, our words have already penetrated into eternity by our Lord who always intercedes for us and a Father that always hears His children. After Zacharias had prayed for a child the angel didn't say his prayer was heard, but is.

"But the angel said unto him, Fear not, Zacharias: for thy prayer is heard; and thy wife Elisabeth shall bear thee a son, and thou shalt call his name John." Luke 1:13

Our prayers and intercession stay in the ears of God. Every promise we speak in prayer to our Lord is always answered yes, received into heaven, and returned into this realm in different times of refreshing.

"**For all the promises of God in him are yea, and in him Amen, unto the glory of God by us.**" **2 Corinthians 1:20**

We were originally created to be immortal like Adam who had dominion over time. We've seen this domination available even in the Old Testament. Joshua prayed and time stood still. Isaiah spoke to the Lord for Hezekiah and time went backwards. One day Jesus walked across the sea, and the ship was three to four miles out. When he got on board he dominated time and they got right back to the shore.

"**Then they willingly received him into the boat, and immediately the boat was at the land where they were going.**" **John 6:21 (NKJ)**

Our quality of life is determined by our effective use of time. When we realize the availability of the 'is-ness' of God, we go from the powerful ministry of healing (*that deals with time*), to the miracles of immediacy (*Greek parachrema*) that do not deal with time. When meditating on Hebrews 11:1, you can just stop after the second word: "*Now faith...*"

The miracles that we *haven't* seen in our lifetime can be a hindrance to our 'life giving' meditation if we walk by sight. If we hear reports of a *'never have seen it before'* from an unwelcome, ungodly spirit, or person, we can put that *never*, or event of time into the past (*or sea of forgetfulness*), and welcome the God of change and restoration. Faith always has to go beyond our experience or it's not faith. With the increase in faith, we perceive, believe and receive the *immediacy* of His Presence and the Spirit of now, moving from glory to glory. Because we know we have eternal life abiding in us, we can look into eternity and see ourselves doing miracles and receiving them.

"**These things have I written unto you that believe on the name of the Son of God; that ye may know that ye** have eternal life, and that ye may believe on the name of the Son of God." 1 John 5:13

God is looking for someone who He can show himself mightily. You have been prepared for this time in the kingdom of God that the world has no clue is available for mankind. You are now being prepared for a greater level of testimony that the majority of the human race has not even heard about. The "nevers" in your life are becoming irretrievable history. You are going to a place where the doubts, worries and fears won't touch you or speak to you. The immediacy of the power of God, the sword of the Spirit, has been activated in you by God's Spirit to serve in the kingdom of God. It is time.

"And when he was demanded of the Pharisees, when the kingdom of God should come, he answered them and said, The kingdom of God cometh not with observation: Neither shall they say, Lo here! or, lo there! for, behold, the kingdom of God is within you." Luke 17:20, 21

CHAPTER 8

The Battle of the Kingdom

Before there was sin on earth, there was sin in God's throne room. The angel Lucifer, who covered the throne with another angel, had sparkling jewels that beamed with the light from being in the presence of God. The first fight in the **Kingdom** began with a difference of opinions caused from self-interest and self-magnification. The heart of an arch angel was lifted up because of his beauty. Other angels agreed with his self-rule and followed him. They were attracted by the music that was built within him and the fullness of wisdom. They were attracted with the precious stones that covered him, reflecting the light of an invisible God that was greater than the shining face of Moses when he came down from Mt. Sinai. With another angel, he once covered the place of the mercy seat in the heaven of heavens, as we've seen in Moses duplication of the Ark of the Covenant (*agreement*). These angels of God would never sing together again.

"**You were in Eden, the garden of God; Every precious stone *was* your covering: The sardius, topaz, and diamond, Beryl, onyx, and jasper, Sapphire, turquoise, and emerald with gold. The workmanship of your timbrels and pipes Was prepared for you on the day** you were created. "You *were* the anointed cherub who covers; I established you; You were on the holy mountain of God; You walked back and forth in the midst of fiery stones. You *were* perfect in your ways from the day you were created, Till iniquity was found in you. "By the abundance of your trading You became filled with violence within, And you sinned; Therefore I cast you as a profane thing Out of the mountain of God; And I destroyed you, O covering cherub, From the midst of the fiery stones. " Your heart was lifted up because of your beauty; You corrupted your wisdom for the sake of your splendor; I cast you to the ground, I laid you before kings, That they might gaze at you." Ezekiel 28:13-17 (NKJ)

"How you are fallen from heaven, O Lucifer, son of the morning! *How* you are cut down to the ground, You who weakened the nations! For you have said in your heart: ' I will ascend into heaven, I will exalt my throne above the stars of God; I will also sit on the mount of the congregation On the farthest sides of the north; I will ascend above the heights of the clouds, I will be like the Most High.'" Isaiah 14:12-14 (NKJ)

"And the cherubim shall stretch out *their* wings above, covering the mercy seat with their wings, and they shall face one another; the faces of the cherubim *shall be* toward the mercy seat. You shall put the mercy seat on top of the ark, and in the ark you shall put the Testimony that I will give you. And there I will meet with you, and I will speak with you from above the mercy seat, from between the two cherubim which *are* on the ark of the Testimony, about everything which I will give you in commandment to the children of Israel." Exodus 25:20-22 (NKJ)

"Where were you when I laid the foundations of the earth? Tell *Me,* if you have understanding. Who determined its measurements? Surely you know! Or who stretched the line upon it? To what were its foundations fastened? Or who laid its cornerstone, When the morning stars sang together, And all the sons of God shouted for joy?" Job 38:4-7 (NKJ)

Lucifer was unsatisfied with what he had and became too ambitious, wanting his own plan, instead of the plan of God. His bitterness became a shared agreement to rebel against God's plan for them to serve mankind.

"But to which of the angels said he at any time, Sit on my right hand, until I make thine enemies thy footstool? Are they not all ministering spirits, sent forth to minister for them who shall be heirs of salvation?" Hebrews 1:14

The darkness would never again understand the light. Instead, the brightness of Jesus, who was manifested to destroy his works, told his disciples; *"... I beheld Satan as lightning fall from heaven"* (Luke10:18). And now, Lucifer became forever unnamed and nameless, only recognized as the devil, or part of a group of an organized rebellion, a way of thinking called Satan, the seed of an ungodly way of thinking called "the flesh"

"God is not mocked: for whatsoever a man soweth, that shall he also reap. For he that soweth to his flesh shall of the flesh reap corruption; but he that soweth to the Spirit shall of the Spirit reap life everlasting." Galatians 6:8, 9

Cast down unto the earth, the center of God's eye on the universe, the rebellion entered into the garden of Eden to take over dominion from the earth. Other 'partners' in crime; Hell and Death, would anxiously wait for permission from man to reign over the planet. Death would take the life from the living soul, and hell would open her mouth to receive it.

"Therefore hell hath enlarged herself, and opened her mouth without measure: and their glory, and their multitude, and their pomp, and he that rejoiceth, shall descend into it. And the mean man shall be brought down,

and the mighty man shall be humbled, and the eyes of the lofty shall be humbled" Isaiah 5:14, 15.

Death would rule from the time of Adam without much opposition and Hell would be fired up at another time as we see in these examples:

"Nevertheless death reigned from Adam to Moses, even over them that had not sinned after the similitude of Adam's transgression, who is the figure of him that was to come." Romans 5:14

"For a fire is kindled in My anger, And shall burn to the lowest hell; It shall consume the earth with her increase, And set on fire the foundations of the mountains. 'I will heap disasters on them; I will spend My arrows on them. *They shall be* **wasted with hunger, Devoured by pestilence and bitter destruction; I will also send against them the teeth of beasts, With the poison of serpents of the dust." Deuteronomy 32:22-24 (NKJ)**

Death and Hell would both be awaiting a future destiny to be thrown into **the lake of fire**, prepared for the devil and his angels.

"And death and hell were cast into the lake of fire. This is the second death." Revelation 20:14

Lying spirits and seducing spirits would try to take over the religious world in the land of the living. And still others, who left their own habitation, have the same expectation for judgment.

"And the angels which kept not their first estate, but left their own habitation, he hath reserved in everlasting chains under darkness unto the judgment of the great day." Jude 1:6

When Adam fell away God, the event tugged upon the heartstrings of the Lord. The tears of God would again be repeated when murder would strike Abel, whose very blood cried from the ground. The perfect plan of redemption, meticulously made well in advance of these events, would release any captives from the temporary prisons of the enemy. God would see the faith that pleases Him, and wipe away all tears.

"**And God shall wipe away all tears from their eyes; and there shall be no more death, neither sorrow, nor crying, neither shall there be any more pain: for the former things are passed away.**" Revelation 21:4

The plan of God to destroy the seed of the serpent, was given to Adam, shown in detail to Enoch, and while they still walked the earth, the 'baton' of faith was passed to his great-grandson Noah, then to the evangelist Abraham (*he was 57 when Noah died*), and spread by word of mouth by many who prophesied different details of the Messiah, the mighty God, who would be given as a son.

"**And the LORD God said unto the serpent, Because thou hast done this, thou art cursed above all cattle, and above every beast of the field; upon thy belly shalt thou go, and dust shalt thou eat all the days of thy life: And I will put enmity between thee and the woman, and between thy seed and her seed; it shall bruise thy head, and thou shalt bruise his heel.**" Genesis 3:14, 15

"**For unto us a child is born, unto us a son is given: and the government shall be upon his shoulder: and his name shall be called Wonderful, Counsellor, The mighty God, The everlasting Father, The Prince of Peace.**" Isaiah 9:6.

Gabriel, who stood in the presence of God, rejoiced with the Lord and his holy angels when the time came to deliver the message of the coming Messiah to Mary, of the Word being made flesh on earth within her. When the Son entered the womb of Mary, her greetings would fill people with the Holy Spirit.

"**And it came to pass, that, when Elisabeth heard the salutation of Mary, the babe leaped in her womb; and Elisabeth was filled with the Holy Ghost**" Luke 1:41

Although Satan would make an attempt to destroy the Messiah at the earliest stages, at any cost, a higher ranking destiny would be fulfilled.

"And when they were departed, behold, the angel of the Lord appeareth to Joseph in a dream, saying, Arise, and take the young child and his mother, and flee into Egypt, and be thou there until I bring thee word: for Herod will seek the young child to destroy him. When he arose, he took the young child and his mother by night, and departed into Egypt... Then Herod, when he saw that he was mocked of the wise men, was exceeding wroth, and sent forth, and slew all the children that were in Bethlehem.." Matthew 2:13-16

When John the Baptist prepared the way for the kingdom of heaven, the kingdom endured violence *until* Jesus came with the activity of the Holy Spirit.

"And from the days of John the Baptist until now the kingdom of heaven suffereth violence, and the violent take it by force." Matthew 11:12

As soon as a voice from heaven proclaimed *"This is my beloved Son,"* the promise of guardian angels returning to fulfill the individual charge of keeping us was tested in the wilderness by Satan.

"And he brought him to Jerusalem, and set him on a pinnacle of the temple, and said unto him, If thou be the Son of God, cast thyself down from hence: For it is written, He shall give his angels charge over thee, to keep thee: And in their hands they shall bear thee up, lest at any time thou dash thy foot against a stone." Luke 4:9, 10

On the word of God, the devil has trembled and ran ever since, knowing that the little ones of God, always have the backup power of Holy angels, ready to bind up demonic spirits as soon as Jesus gave away keys (*delegated authority*) to the kingdom of heaven (Matt 16:19).

"Thou believest that there is one God; thou doest well: the devils also believe, and tremble." James 2:19

"Submit yourselves therefore to God. Resist the devil, and he will flee from you." James 4:7

"Take heed that ye despise not one of these little ones; for I say unto you, That in heaven their angels do always behold the face of my Father which is in heaven." Matthew 18:10

"And I will give unto thee the keys of the kingdom of heaven: and whatsoever thou shalt bind on earth shall be bound in heaven: and whatsoever thou shalt loose on earth shall be loosed in heaven." Matthew 16:19

From then on, every man would press into the kingdom of God through the name (*authority*) of Jesus, and once again, the spirits became subject to men. And if we need a legions of angels, we now have the power with the Word the same as Jesus, so we are not just talk, but have actions that speak louder than words, noted in these verses:

"The law and the prophets were until John: since that time the kingdom of God is preached, and every man presseth into it." Luke 16:16

"And the seventy returned again with joy, saying, Lord, even the devils are subject unto us through thy name. And he said unto them, I beheld Satan as lightning fall from heaven. Behold, I give unto you power to tread on serpents and scorpions, and over all the power of the enemy: and nothing shall by any means hurt you." Luke 10:17-19

".. because as he is (*Jesus*), so are we in this world." 1 John 4:17

"But ye are come unto mount Sion, and unto the city of the living God, the heavenly Jerusalem, and to an innumerable company of angels" Hebrews 12:22

"And my speech and my preaching was not with enticing words of man's wisdom, but in demonstration of the Spirit and of power" 1 Corinthians 2:4

When Jesus laid down his life, three different apostles tell us how he descended into hell, preached in prison, taking the keys of death and hell, and made a spectacle of them.

"Now that he ascended, what is it but that he also descended first into the lower parts of the earth?" Ephesians 4:10

"For Christ also suffered once for sins, the just for the unjust, that He might bring us to God, being put to death in the flesh but made alive by the Spirit, by whom also He went and preached to the spirits in prison" 1 Peter 3:18, 19 (NKJ)

"I am he that liveth, and was dead; and, behold, I am alive for evermore, Amen; and have the keys of hell and of death." Revelation 1:19

"Having disarmed principalities and powers, He made a public spectacle of them, triumphing over them in it." Colossians 2:15 (NKJ)

The enemy watched in horror as His angel rolled the stone from his grave in the presence of the Roman soldiers, who shook and fell out as He rose from the grave. The secular guardsmen would be among the first to testify of His resurrection.

"And behold, there was a great earthquake; for an angel of the Lord descended from heaven, and came and rolled back the stone from the door, and sat on it. His countenance was like lightning and his clothing as white as snow. And the guards shook for fear of him, and became like dead *men*." Matthew 28:2-4 (NKJ)

On the way to heaven, on his *first* ascension, He briefly spoke to Martha, who could not touch Him, until He took his own royal blood into the heaven of heavens, in the same manner of old Levitical priests. At the time, heaven's throne room was still stained with the sin of the fallen angels, but His own royal blood was paid for us, so now we can go boldly to the throne of grace, sitting together with Him in heavenly places, ever interceding for us, inside us:

"**Jesus saith unto her, Touch me not; for I am not yet ascended to my Father: but go to my brethren, and say unto them, I ascend unto my Father, and your Father; and to my God, and your God.**" John 20:17

"**Neither by the blood of goats and calves, but by his own blood he entered in once into the holy place, having obtained eternal redemption for us.**" Hebrews 9:12

"**For Christ is not entered into the holy places made with hands, which are the figures of the true; but into heaven itself, now to appear in the presence of God for us**" Hebrews 9:24

"**Wherefore he is able also to save them to the uttermost that come unto God by him, seeing he ever liveth to make intercession for them.**" Hebrews 7:25

If the princes of this *world* could see this coming, they would've never arranged for His death. If they could have seen Him setting the captives free and many bodies of the saints coming out of the graves after His resurrection, they would have known He was more powerful having an experience with death than an experience with life. For now, the prince of the world was cast out.

"**Which none of the princes of this world knew: for had they known it, they would not have crucified the Lord of glory.**" 1 Corinthians 2:8

"**And the graves were opened; and many bodies of the saints which slept arose, and came out of the graves after his resurrection, and went into the holy city, and appeared unto many.**" Matthew 27:52, 53

"**Now is the judgment of this world: now shall the prince of this world be cast out.**" John 12:32

On the *second* ascension, after being seen by over 500 people at one time, the battle of the Kingdom would intensify.

"After that, he was seen of above five hundred brethren at once; of whom the greater part remain unto this present, but some are fallen asleep." 1Corinthians 15:6

The power of Jesus would magnify exponentially, from a small corner of the world like a mustard seed, into a planet of believers from the greatest tree of life, enabling power on the planet. The inheritance of the saints was the rule of the Kingdom, through the power of the Holy Spirit, bought with the price of God's own blood.

"...feed the church of God, which he hath purchased with his own blood." Acts 20:28

The believers of God, or the body of Christ, have been given the "power of attorney," or the responsibility to be representatives of authority over the Kingdom, and jurisdiction over all things.

"But as many as received him, to them gave he power to become the sons of God, even to them that believe on his name" John 1:13

"Therefore let no man glory in men. For all things are yours; whether Paul, or Apollos, or Cephas, or the world, or life, or death, or things present, or things to come; all are yours" 1 Corinthians 3:21, 22

The Father freely granted to His children the anointing on the earth, and the power for the restoration and correction of all things that were wrong. The greatest miracle is an eternal life with the Everlasting Father with their names written in heaven. Surely, the *lesser* miracles are easier to receive.

The unraveling of the thousands of years of lies of the enemy and the traditions of religion was next on the agenda for the battle of the Kingdom. A new ministry of apostles, prophets, evangelists, pastors and teachers would be sent for the equipping and perfecting of the saints, and the unity of the body of Christ. The Lamb of God will only accept

The final battle of the Kingdom will have the rejoicing of all creation.

"For I reckon that the sufferings of this present time are not worthy to be compared with the glory which shall be revealed in us. For the earnest expectation of the creature waiteth for the manifestation of the sons of God. For the creature was made subject to vanity, not willingly, but by reason of him who hath subjected the same in hope, Because the creature itself also shall be delivered from the bondage of corruption into the glorious liberty of the children of God." Romans 8:18-21

God will rejoice over us and sing, the mountains joining in the chorus; while the trees of the clap their hands.

"The LORD your God in your midst, The Mighty One, will save; He will rejoice over you with gladness, He will quiet *you* with His love, He will rejoice over you with singing." Zephaniah 3:17 (NKJ)

"For you shall go out with joy, and be led forth with peace: the mountains and hills shall break forth before you into singing, and all the tress of the field shall clap their hands" Isaiah 55:12

CHAPTER 9

The Mystery of the Kingdom

It has always been God's desire to share the secrets of the Kingdom with us.

"The secret things belong unto the Lord our God: but those things which are revealed belong unto us and our children for ever... " Deuteronomy 29:29

"And he said unto them, Unto you it is given to know the mystery of the kingdom of God: but unto them that are without, all these things are done in parables" Mark 4:11

The only thing that covers the information, is the devil, who will attempt to cover up the truth with his own words, or immediately steal a word that has been planted into us (Mark 4:15). Since we can only serve one master at a time, we will listen to him, or listen to what is revealed by God.

"In whom the god of this world hath blinded the minds of them which believe not, lest the light of the glorious gospel of Christ, who is the image of God, should shine unto them" 2 Corinthians 4:4

The Spirit of God is one who uncovers, or reveals the Truth, the Word of God.

"Now to him that is of power to stablish you according to my gospel, and the preaching of Jesus Christ, according to the revelation of the mystery, which was kept secret since the world began, but now is made manifest, and by the scriptures of the prophets, according to the commandment of the everlasting God, made known to all nations for the obedience of faith" Romans 16:25, 26

The developing stages of the believers of the Word went from being in the "womb" in the Old Testament, to a newborn body of Christ, into maturity. In each stage, mysteries were revealed by layers, until all the counsel of God had been revealed by His Holy Spirit.

"That their hearts might be comforted, being knit together in love, and unto all riches of the full assurance of understanding, to the acknowledgement of the mystery of God, and of the Father, and of Christ; In whom are hid all the treasures of wisdom and knowledge." Colossians 2:3

"For I have not shunned to declare unto you all the counsel of God." Acts 20:27

Isaiah, David and other prophets proclaimed bits and pieces of mysteries that were coming way beyond their lifetime on earth.

"Therefore the Lord himself shall give you a sign; Behold, a virgin shall conceive, and bear a son, and shall call his name Immanuel" Isaiah 7:14

"The LORD said unto my Lord, Sit thou at my right hand, until I make thine enemies thy footstool" Psalm 110:1

"Behold I send you Elijah the prophet before the coming of the great and dreadful day of the Lord" Malachi 4:5, 6

They all carried "concealed" weapons, but could personally see things when the Spirit came upon them. When John the Baptist came, he prepared a way for the coming of the Messiah in the flesh. When Jesus came, He prepared a way for the indwelling of the Holy Spirit in us. Thus, in general, the Old Testament was written with many previews or shadows of the Word.

"Which are a shadow of things to come; but the body is of Christ." Colossians 2:17

Many people are in different growth stages in the body of Christ. When we reach different levels of maturity, Jesus reveals to us things that He always intended for us to know; the mystery of His will (which is His word), so that we can be one with Him.

"Having made known unto us the mystery of his will, according to his good pleasure which he hath purposed in himself" Ephesians 1:9

"If ye have heard of the dispensation of the grace of God which is given me to you-ward: How that by revelation he made known unto me the mystery; (as I wrote afore in few words, whereby, when ye read, ye may understand my knowledge in the mystery of Christ) which in other ages was not made known unto the sons of men, as it is now revealed unto his holy apostles and prophets by the Spirit" Ephesians 3:2-5

Some spiritual 'babes' can only handle milk, not being used to being fed only by God, but are still slowly being weaned from the world.

"And I, brethren, could not speak to you as to spiritual *people* but as to carnal, as to babes in Christ. I fed you with milk and not with solid food; for unto now you were not able *to receive it*, and even now you are still not able." 1 Corinthians 3:1, 2 (NKJ)

Some children can only handle "honey", but the sons can handle the meat.

"For everyone who partakes *only* of milk *is* unskilled in the word of righteousness, for he is a babe. But solid food belongs to those who are of full age, *that is,* those who by reason of use have their senses exercised to discern both good and evil." Hebrews 5:13, 14 (NKJ)

The fathers in the faith give it out with patience consistency.

"Take heed therefore unto yourselves, and to all the flock, over the which the Holy Ghost hath made you overseers, to feed the church of God..." Acts 20:28

When Jesus was walking with his disciples, they enjoyed an Immanuel, which was God with us, but His mission was to prepare for God in us.

"Jesus answered and said unto him, If a man love me, he will keep my words: and my Father will love him, and we will come unto him, and make our abode with him." John 14:24

At that time, it was only given to them to know the mysteries of God. His plan was not to have people confident in the flesh, or the seen world, who would want to make the "image" of God king, but that the faith in the unseen would rule.

"When Jesus therefore perceived that they would come and take him by force, to make him a king, he departed again into a mountain himself alone." John 6:15

His plan was to have us corporately grow in time from spiritual babes to mature and patient adults, having confidence in the dominion He originally gave to us. Since the fall of man, this requires quite a long time, which included the prophets prophesying, John's teaching, The Lord's coming, the Spirit leading, and even a millennium period before all of the needed time is fulfilled. They didn't want Him to leave, but were not able to grasp the few clues to what it would be like with Him *in* them, instead of near Him.

"However, when He, the Spirit of truth, has come, He will guide you into all truth; for He will not speak on His own *authority*, but whatever He hears He will speak; and He will tell you things to come." John 16:12, 13 (NKJ)

The examples of how to live a Godly life of dominion were performed in His life, so that we could relate to the Spirit of God working upon us, were important, but pales in the comparison of the Spirit *in* us, to do greater works.

"Most assuredly, I say to you, he who believes in Me, the works that I do he will do also; and greater *works* than these he will do, because I go to My Father." John 14:12 (NKJ)

In Paul's letters, he repeatedly uncovered the mystery of the Kingdom and solicited prayer for bold utterance to declare the mystery of the gospel.

"Even the mystery which hath been hid from ages and from generations, but now is made manifest to his saints: To whom God would make known what is the riches of the glory of this mystery among the Gentiles; <u>which is Christ in you</u>, the hope of glory Whom we preach, warning every man, and teaching every man in all wisdom; that we may present every man perfect in Christ Jesus" Colossians 1:26-28

Because we are justified and glorified to take on the divine nature of Him *in* us, we can look at our prayer life and spiritual walk in a different, more personal way.

"According as his divine power hath given unto us all things that pertain unto life and godliness, through the knowledge of him that hath called us to glory and virtue: Whereby are given unto us exceeding great and precious promises: that by these ye might be partakers of the divine nature, having escaped the corruption that is in the world through lust." 2 Peter 1:3, 4

So many people now pray and think of an impersonal "far-away" God or an "up there" God, whose desire was not just to come by and visit, or stand at the door and knock, but His heart longed to be alive *in* us with all life, peace and wisdom.

"For this cause we also, since the day we heard it, do not cease to pray for you, and to desire that ye might be

filled with the knowledge of his will in all wisdom and spiritual understanding" Colossians 1:9

Even when we have rejected His ways before out of ignorance, the adversary was defeated, so that even now we could boldly go to the throne of grace and dwell in the secret place of the Most High. Even if 1,000 people around us fall, or 10,000 right by us because they don't know the mystery of Christ and His divine protection, it will not come near us. With Christ *in* us, Hell shakes when we pray with God's living Words coming out of our mouths. The demons back away from the Holy ground we walk on, resulting in the promise of long life that God wants to satisfy us with.

When we have our own personal 'rapture' and sit in heavenly places *in* Christ, we find ourselves being *in* Him, far above all principality, dominion and might.

"Which he wrought in Christ, when he raised him from the dead, and set him at his own right hand in the heavenly places, far above all principality, and power, and might, and dominion, and every name that is named, not only in this world, but also in that which is to come" Ephesians 1:20, 21

"And hath raised us up together, and made us sit together in heavenly places in Christ Jesus" Ephesians 2:6

As we are perfected, as Jesus our master,

"The disciple is not above his master: but every one that is perfect shall be as his master." Luke 6:40

Who didn't find Himself wrong to be equal with God, because as He IS, so are WE in the world (1 John 4:17).

When we show up, God shows up. When we realize our 'oneness' with Jesus, and the availability of the knowledge of God was given to Paul, and other believers as we are all called to know the revelations of His mysteries.

"And I myself also am persuaded of you, my brethren, that ye also are full of goodness, filled with all knowledge, able also to admonish one another." Romans 15:14

"But as it is written, Eye hath not seen, nor ear heard, neither have entered into the heart of man, the things which God hath prepared for them that love him. But God hath revealed them unto us by his Spirit: for the Spirit searcheth all things, yea, the deep things of God." 1 Corinthians 2:9, 10

When we find that God is no respecter of persons, we will use this revelation to do all things through Christ who strengthens us, and consistently perform the miraculous! When we put off the old man and put on Christ, we can be "know-it-all" and "do-it-all" people!

"I can do all things through Christ which strengtheneth me." Philippians 4:13

We will rightfully gather the spoils of the enemy and say the Spirit of the Lord is upon *me* to loose the captives, and reveal in boldness, the mystery of the Kingdom!

CHAPTER 10

The Life of the Kingdom

God's plan has always been for us to have a fulfilling, long life.

"*There shall nothing cast their young, nor be barren, in thy land: the number of thy days I will fulfil.*" **Exodus 23:26**

In the 90th Psalm, Moses makes an observation from experience in verse 10: "*The days of our years are 70; and if by reason of strength they be 80 years.*" In verse 12, he makes a request for wisdom: "*So teach us to number our days, that we may apply our hearts unto wisdom.*"

After talking with the Lord, he proves that experience is not the best teacher, but His Spirit teaches us how to walk by faith and not by sight, for he himself lived for 120 years (Deut 34:7), going back to God's word in Genesis 6:3:

"**And the LORD said, My spirit shall not always strive with man, for that he also is flesh: yet his days shall be an hundred and twenty years.**"

In the next Psalm, 91:16 the Spirit rightfully claims "*With long life I will satisfy him...*" Staying in the secret place of the Lord will keep you, even if 10,000 fall at your side or don't take hold of the promises available for all (Ps 91:9-11).

The 'clues' or pathways have been written in the Word throughout the Old Testament. In Exodus 20:12, it says to honor your mother and father that your days will be long upon the earth. A lifestyle of obedience to your first authority makes it easier to obey your Father in heaven for your spiritual protection and longevity.

""Honor your father and mother," which is the first commandment with promise: that it may be well with you and you may live long on the earth." Ephesians 6:2, 3 (NKJ)

This scripture of obedience is parallel to other figures of authority (Heb 13:7/Col 3:22). The centurion with the sick servant knew how to capitalize on the way authority works, with the promise of life in the kingdom (Matt 8:9, 10). If he got a Word on it, that's all he needed. The same applies to us. We have dominion over distance. The Word is not bound! Having the applicable wisdom of God's commandments will give us long life, health and peace.

"...let your heart keep my commands; For length of days and long life And peace they will add to you." Proverbs 3:1, 2

"The fear of the LORD *is* the beginning of wisdom, And the knowledge of the Holy One *is* understanding. For by me your days will be multiplied, and years of life will be added to you" Proverbs 9:10, 11 (NKJ)

Of course, keeping away from strange women and evil men breaks off our hold on the pathways of life, as would a greedy life (Proverbs 2:16-19, 4:10-14, 5:5 and 28:16). We even have power in our mouth to bring life or death.

"Death and life are in the power of the tongue: and they that love it will eat its fruit." Proverbs 18:21 (NKJ)

Some lose out by ignorance of the promises.

"My people are destroyed for lack of knowledge..." Hosea 4:6

The promises of the devil tell us about a short life, or we never know when we'll go, they come in threes, or even the accusing; "God took them away," when it is written, he is the one who came to *"steal kill and destroy"* (John 10:10).

Sad stories may even come from pulpits.

"As we said before, so say I now again, If any man preach any other gospel unto you than that ye have received, let him be accursed." Galatians 1:9

Agreement with the enemy can cause a shepherd to bury you early or you burying them. When we are ready and have done what we have been called to do, we should simply "pass away".

For a long life in the kingdom, we need to have vision, purpose and faithfulness for health, youthfulness, goodness and mercy to follow us.

"Where there is no vision, the people perish: but he that keepeth the law, happy is he." Proverbs 29:18

"Who (*God*) satisfies your mouth with good *things, so that* your youth is renewed like the eagle's." Psalms 103:5 (NKJ)

Our days should be heavenly.

"That your days may be multiplied, and the days of your children, in the land which the LORD sware unto your fathers to give them, as the days of heaven upon the earth." Deuteronomy 11:21

Renewing our strength like the eagles is for now, not when we step into immortal life.

"But they that wait upon the LORD shall renew their strength; they shall mount up with wings as eagles; they shall run, and not be weary; and they shall walk, and not faint." Isaiah 40:31

We should desire a strong life like Caleb.

"And now, behold, the LORD hath kept me alive, as he said, these 45 years...and now, lo, I am this day 85 years old. As yet I am as strong this day as I was in the

day that Moses sent me: as my strength was then, even so is my strength now, for war, both to go out, and to come in." Josh 14:10, 11

In the areas where we are weak in, we should find a Word for our answer and meditate on it until we are in cooperation with the Spirit, so that the weak can say; I'm strong. No weapon formed against us shall prosper. No plague shall befall us. No one takes our life unless we give it. (*see, in this order*, Joel 3:10; Is 54:17; Ps 91:10; 1 John 5:17; and, John 10:18)

Many have "fallen asleep" who have not discerned the Lord's body.

"For he who eats and drinks in an unworthy manner eats and drinks judgment to himself, not discerning the Lord's body. For this reason many *are* weak and sick among you, and many sleep." 1 Corinthians 11:29, 30 (NKJ)

In all truths being parallel, there should be discernment of the body of Christ and its different members. When you can discern and receive a prophet, you'll get a prophets reward (Matt 10:41). If someone gives you a Word from the Head of the church for your life and you don't take it as such, you could miss out on your abundance. Even the small prompting from within our spirit to lead us and guide us, are there for life preserving agreement with His Word. When you hear the available promises of life from the Word, and realize the reason for us staying here successfully is to build the Kingdom, we can be assured that God wants to fulfill His promise through us. The "good fight of faith" is the fight that you're winning. There is only victory in the kingdom.

"Beloved, I pray that you may prosper in all thins and be in health, just as your soul prospers." 3 John 1:3 (NKJ)

Live long and prosper, in the life of the Kingdom.

CHAPTER 11

The Possibilities of the Kingdom

There possibilities in the Kingdom are unlimited. The limits we usually have are the ones we give ourselves, or the circumstances and experiences we trust rather than God's Word.

"...The things which are impossible with men are possible with God." Luke 18:28

The prophets, including John, pointed to a day when the Messiah would come. When He came, Jesus pointed to a day when the God would come in us. After Immanuel was God incarnate walking on the earth, His promise was to send another Comforter to be *in* us with the addition of the Father and Son, or full Godhead, to make God Incarnate in us.

"But the Comforter, which is the Holy Ghost, whom the Father will send in my name, he shall teach you all things, and bring all things to your remembrance, whatsoever I have said unto you." John 14:26

God has chosen us to have God incarnate in us, or GIs, soldiers for Christ with His whole armour, sword, and faith that pleases Him.

"No one engaged in warfare entangles himself with the affairs of *this* life, that he may please him who enlisted him as a soldier." 2 Timothy 2:4 (NKJ)

God has made us His house, temple and tabernacle. He moved in with all His faith, power and wisdom, available for us when we decide to let Him live and not us. In the Old Testament days, people got miracles on credit. If we were to do a "credit check" now, we would find the blood has already been paid in full for our inheritance. We can stake our claim through His Spirit and confirm it with His Word.

God *looks* for people who know what to expect from Him.

"When Jesus heard it, he marvelled, and said to them that followed, Verily I say unto you, I have not <u>found</u> so great faith, no, not in Israel." Matthew 8:10

For all who ask receive.

"Ask, and it will be given to you; seek, and you will find; knock, and it will be opened to you. For everyone who asks receives, and he who seeks finds, and to him who knocks it will be opened." Matthew 7:7, 8 (NKJ)

When we know His nature and His Will, we receive confidence in what He will do for us and through us as an everlasting Father of love, compassion, faith and power. He repeatedly gave us the opportunity to ask for anything to build the kingdom of God and gather the spoils of the enemy, as seen here in the Greek scholar Kenneth S. Weust's expanded translation:

"And all things, whatever you shall ask in prayer, believing, you shall receive." Matthew 21:22 (KW)

"And whatever ye shall ask in my Name, this will I do, in order that the Father may be glorified in the Son. If ye shall ask any thing in my Name, I will do it." John 14:13, 14 (KW)

"You did not make me the object of your choice for yourselves, but I selected you out for myself, and I appointed you in order that you might be going away and constantly bearing fruit, and that your fruit might be remaining, in order that whatever you might ask the

Father in my Name, He may give it you" John 15:16 (KW)

"...Most assuredly, I am saying to you, Whatever you shall request of the Father, He will give it to you in view of all that I am in His estimation." John 16:23 (KW)

Some of us are not used to the possibilities with God and may doubt as we have come out of a world dependent upon circumstances, walking by sight and not by faith, or ask for selfish reasons.

"But let him ask in faith, with no doubting, for he who doubts is like a wave of the sea driven and tossed by the wind. For let not that man suppose that he will receive anything from the Lord" James 1:6, 7 (NKJ)

"You ask and do not receive, because you ask amiss, that you may spend *it* on your pleasures." James 4:3 (NKJ)

If we need more faith, the way to get it is to hear more word, and decrease the listening of unfruitful or ungodly words. If we ask the Lord to 'help our unbelief' or help us in areas that we haven't received a solid promise on yet, we can listen to the Spirit for direction, and meditate on the confirmations in the Word that He gives us Himself or His called preachers. We are not called to live in mediocrity, just getting by or hanging in there. God is ready and waiting to make our joy full and go beyond our expectations.

"Now unto him that is able to do exceeding abundantly above all that we ask or think, according to the power that worketh in us" Ephesians 3:20

When we were first born again, we had a great confidence in His power and had many early prayers fulfilled. Though religion and many sermons have taught limitations and mediocrity, God Himself is reviving our spirits above the modern day Pharisees, and chosen frozen, who are never able to grow to another level.

There is no power outside Kingdom power

"But woe unto you, scribes and Pharisees, hypocrites! for ye shut up the kingdom of heaven against men: for ye neither go in yourselves, neither suffer ye them that are entering to go in." Matthew 23:13

We know what to expect from Him, when we read His Word, and we find out what He desires us to do. He chooses us and uses us by what we believe (*our faith*). When we are in agreement with His ways, the desires of His hearts become the desires of ours.

"**Delight thyself also in the LORD; and he shall give you the desires of thine heart. Commit your way unto the LORD; trust also in him; and he shall bring it to pass**" Psalms 37:4, 5

When we have great faith, we are spiritually thrust out as pioneers, fully backed up with the power of the Word, as many fathers of faith were in the bible. When the information of the bible becomes living revelation that the Spirit gives to us, our heavenly identity is revealed, and we can walk in power and in truth.

The devil has a false, 'make believe' temporary world that he wants us to believe or have faith in, but Jesus gave us master keys to all things pertaining to life, so that we can gather the spoils from the enemy, or bring back what the devil has stolen from the body of Christ. God wants us to experience a reputation with His life on it. Even when we do bold things, some people may have a fear of this mystery, even as the people around the man possessed with the legion of demons did, or the disciples feared when Jesus walked on the water. When we have uncovered the power within us, miracles in our lives become commonplace and our daily expectations. Has God spoken and is His Word untrue? Oh no! His Word is His bond. When you reverence God and take Him at His Word at face value, you enter into His power realm, where all things are possible.

"God is not a man that he should lie; neither the son of man that he should repent: hath he said, and shall he not do it? or hath he spoken, and shall he not make it good?" Numbers 23:19

Heaven must respond to our prayers when we meet the criteria of the bible.

"If you maintain a living communion with me and my words are at home in you, I command you to ask, at once, something for yourself, whatever your heart desires, and it will become yours" John 15:7 (KW)

The reason we can ask anything in the name of Jesus is to glorify His name on the earth, build His kingdom, and that our joy may be full.

"Herein is my Father glorified, that ye bear much fruit; so shall ye be my disciples." John 15:8

"These things have I spoken unto you, that my joy might remain in you, and that your joy might be full." John15:12

"God be merciful to us, and bless us; and cause his face to shine upon us; That thy way may be known upon the earth, thy saving health among the nations" Psalm 67:1, 2

Our joy will be really full joy when, when above all things, our brothers and sisters are healed, prosperous and have full knowledge of His name and nature.

"Beloved, in all things I am praying that you will be prospering, and that you will be continually having good health just as your soul is prospering" 3 John 1:3 (KW)

Because there is nothing impossible with God, we can go into this dimension to have whatever we ask. It becomes natural to be super-natural and perform miracles. When people tell us about their concerns, we can say "You don't have to worry about it, I'm about to pray!"

"And he said, The things which are impossible with men are possible with God." Luke 18:27

We have an **unction** from God, so our confession will become our daily provision. When we speak boldly in His name, He will always show up. We already have the Truth; we just need to hold onto it (Heb 3:6). The greatest miracle is for us to unflinchingly hold on unto this Word, and spread this confidence throughout the world.

"But Christ as a son over his own house; whose house are we, if we hold fast the confidence and the rejoicing of the hope firm unto the end." Hebrews 3:6

All things are not only possible with the Kingdom, but will happen, because God answers prayer!

"Let us hold fast the profession of our faith without wavering; (for he is faithful that promised)" Hebrews 10:23

CHAPTER 12

The Finances of the Kingdom

"The silver is mine, and the gold is mine, saith the LORD of hosts." Haggai 2:8
The earth is the Lord's and all that is in it.
"...all things were created by him, and <u>for</u> him" Colossians 1:16
It has always been His intention for us to enjoy the fruit of the land, the fruit of our labors, the works of our hands and all the riches available on this planet to share as a family. Because the love of money is the root of all evil, we've seen the earliest root of the enemy who was covered with jewels, position, and authority and became greedy and wanted more.
"You were in Eden, the garden of God; Every precious stone *was* your covering...turquoise...emerald...gold... You were on the holy mountain of God...you were created, Till iniquity was found in you." Ezekiel 28:13-15
The system of not sharing, but attempts to steal, kill and destroy had just begun. Jesus proclaimed:
"The thief cometh not, but for to steal, and to kill, and to destroy: I am come that they might have life, and that they might have it more abundantly." John 10:10

Jesus came to restore that which was lost, so that we could reclaim what was His, and ours by inheritance. This included the things to come like streets of gold, gates of pearls and magnificent beauty.

"...For all things are yours; Whether Paul, or Apollos, or Cephas, or the world, or life, or death, or things present, or things to come; all are yours" 1 Corinthians 3:21, 22

The giving of tithes was seen throughout the Old Testament. When the earth received the heart of the Holy Spirit, the acceleration of giving was noted among the apostles. They returned to the original plan of God with unity and sharing, the kingdom way of thinking.

"And the multitude of them that believed were of one heart and of one soul: neither said any of them that ought of the things which he possessed was his own; but they had all things common...Neither was there any among them that lacked: for as many as were possessors of lands or houses sold them, and brought the prices of the things that were sold, And laid them down at the apostles' feet: and distribution was made unto every man according as he had need." Acts 4:32-35

The Aramaic language, in which the original New Testament books were written, contained many idioms (*like in the English, "He's in hot water" means "He's in trouble"*) in common speech and the scriptures. The idiom for *"At the feet of the apostles"* means *"Gifts given with no strings attached."* These saints who embraced the kingdom truly gave free-heartedly.

When the kingdom way becomes what we seek first, we get in line with the Word by being a good steward of our finances. It was not intended for us to owe money and have any kind of similar bondage of debt and stress. To be blessed (*empowered to prosper*) is being the lender and not the borrower.

"The rich rules over the poor, And the borrower *is* servant to the lender The rich ruleth over the poor, and the borrower is servant to the lender." Proverbs 22:7 (NKJ)

"For the LORD your God will bless you just as He promised you; you shall lend to many nations, but you shall not borrow; you shall reign over many nations, but they shall not reign over you." Deuteronomy 15:6 (NKJ)

When we are givers and think first about the kingdom, our containers will overflow.

"Honor the LORD with your possessions, And with the firstfruits of all your increase; So your barns will be filled with plenty, And your vats will overflow with new wine." Proverbs 3:9, 10

The kingdom way of living can go even higher than many think. It is best to possess the land and not make payments. The paths climb higher and higher, so that wealth and riches follow us like goodness and mercy. Righteous Lot followed his blessings and had wealth by association. Holy Abraham, the faithful friend of God had the blessings follow him. He was very rich and showed favor, with the blessings promised to his descendents. Jesus took us away from the curse of poverty and gave us the blessings of Abraham by faith. We should not forget we are blessed to be a blessing.

"So it shall be, when the LORD your God brings you into the land of which He swore to your fathers, to Abraham, Isaac, and Jacob, to give you large and beautiful cities which you did not build, houses full of all good things, which you did not fill, hewn-out wells which you did not dig, vineyards and olive trees which you did not plant—when you have eaten and are full— *then* beware, lest you forget the LORD who brought you out of the land of Egypt, from the house of bondage." Deuteronomy 6:10-12 (NKJ)

"Wealth and riches shall be in his house..." Psalm 112:3

"Christ hath redeemed us from the curse of the law, being made a curse for us... that the blessing of Abraham might come on the Gentiles through Jesus Christ; that we might receive the promise of the Spirit through faith." Galatians 3:13, 14

Our prosperity is readily available and will manifest where we have planted that particular kind of 'seed' and listen to the promptings of God, and those who truly speak on His behalf. Of course, we should pay our debts (*or try not to make any*) first, and leave that bondage, and be free to give our first and our best to the house of God. We don't give to get blessed; we give because we are blessed.

"...Believe in the LORD your God, so shall ye be established; believe his prophets, so shall ye prosper." 2 Chronicles 20:20

When we prosper, we make the kingdom look rightfully attractive to those outside (*as it should*). The fairness, joy and peace of this attitude is how God wants to show us off to the world for His glory. Although some are content with the basics, or have not yet mastered receiving for the blessing of the kingdom, God wants the world to know that He knows how to take care of His children.

"God be merciful unto us, and bless us...That thy way may be known upon earth, thy saving health among all nations." Psalm 67:1, 2

"...Let the LORD be magnified, which hath pleasure in the prosperity of his servant." Psalm 35:27

"...remember the LORD thy God: for it is he that giveth thee power to get wealth, that he may establish his covenant which he sware unto thy fathers, as it is this day." Deuteronomy 8:18

Don't be afraid of having billions if your heart is giving, because there are many people in need. Even Jesus Himself started His journey with an offering of gold, had the family skills of a carpenter, kept money for distribution to the poor, and had the burial of a rich man. God gives seed to the sower. When our trust is in the source instead of the money, and we don't have 'sticky fingers' we are rich by faith.

"Charge them that are rich in this world, that they be not highminded, nor trust in uncertain riches, but in the living God, who giveth us richly all things to enjoy; That they do good, that they be rich in good works, ready to distribute, willing to communicate; Laying up in store for themselves a good foundation against the time to come, that they may lay hold on eternal life." 1 Timothy 6:17-19

In the kingdom, we are on our mission for the great transference of wealth. It is God's plan to reconcile all things with Him. His plan is already started to take the spoils of the enemy, including wealth of all kinds, including television and radio media, banks and buildings that should be used for His purpose, in the near future.

"…and the wealth of the sinner is laid up for the just." Proverbs 13:22

"…and the wealth of all the heathen round about shall be gathered together, gold, and silver, and apparel, in great abundance." Zechariah 14:14

We know that Jesus said we could ask anything in His name including finances, as it will take money to make the gospel available to all the earth. Ask for the benefit of the kingdom. Prepare to spoil the enemy like the children of Israel spoiled the Egyptians into a land of rest. Prepare for a land with sharing and caring. Prepare to be used financially for the benefit of the kingdom.

"The blessing of the LORD, it makes one rich, And He adds no sorrow with it." Proverbs 10:22 (NKJ)

CHAPTER 13

The Angels of the Kingdom

The angels of the kingdom serve a significant purpose in the kingdom of God. They are mentioned in the New Testament many more times than the old covenant. When we learn how to cooperate with them, their assignments of ministry to us are much easier.

"Behold, I send an Angel before you to keep you in the way and to bring you into the place which I have prepared. Beware of Him and obey His voice; do not provoke Him, for He will not pardon your transgressions; for My name *is* in Him" Exodus 23:20, 21

Their lives in the activity of the believer guide and help those who are to inherit salvation, by helping us perform the word. We no longer have to rely on them for a 'word of knowledge' since we have the Holy Spirit within us, but they are still very much active in our lives. They are in agreement with God's word and love to obey, while the bad angels have to obey because of the force of Light. The glory of the Lord in us attracts both sides, so we should stay in the presence of God. His holy angels are on assignment to make sure you get your blessing. They harken to the voice of the Lord, even if it comes from you (Psalm 103:20). They are curious creatures that wonder what it's like to have God pleasing faith in a Creator someone who has never seen. They minister to us, being sent by God. They are holy, seeking first the kingdom of God, and always act parallel to the Word.

"But to which of the angels said he at any time, Sit on my right hand, until I make thine enemies thy footstool? Are they not all ministering spirits, sent forth to minister for them who shall be heirs of salvation?" **Hebrews 1:13, 14**

"The LORD hath prepared his throne in the heavens; and his kingdom ruleth over all. Bless the LORD, ye his angels, that excel in strength, that do his commandments, hearkening unto the voice of his word. Bless ye the LORD, all ye his hosts; ye ministers of his, that do his pleasure." **Psalm 103:19-21**

We are more than conquerors. God is the Lord of hosts or armies, and His holy angels outnumber the evil angels two to one.

"And his *(Satan's)* tail drew the third part of the stars of heaven, and did cast them to the earth.." **Revelation 12:4.**

"But where sin abounded, grace did much more abound" **Romans 5:20**

Jesus encountered a legion of demons and was not impressed, but cast them out. He said that angels ascend and descend upon Him. They always protect people with purpose. They are not in heaven protecting God, but are here on earth sent out on our behalf, whether we notice them or not.

"And he answered, Fear not: for they that be with us are more than they that be with them. And Elisha prayed, and said, LORD, I pray thee, open his eyes, that he may see. And the LORD opened the eyes of the young man; and he saw: and, behold, the mountain was full of horses and chariots of fire round about Elisha." **2 Kings 6:16, 17.**

"For he shall give his angels charge over you, To keep you in all your ways." Psalm 91:11 (NKJ)
Some have been with them without knowing.
"Be not forgetful to entertain strangers: for thereby some have entertained angels unawares." Hebrews 13:2
The angels of the Lord are part of an innumerable powerful army. One angel single-handedly thousands in one night.
"Then the angel of the LORD went forth, and smote in the camp of the Assyrians a hundred and fourscore and five thousand: and when they arose early in the morning, behold, they were all dead corpses." Isaiah 37:36
Angels work with us and for us. Angels are like heavenly 'bouncers' to eject devils for us. They rejoice and show up in numbers when you speak the Word of God with boldness. When you talk about the immediacies of God with expectancy, they surround you like a wall. When you are in your house interceding, big angels are packed in it like sardines. They are ready to break chains off of you and get you out of prison if necessary, just so can proclaim the Word and lead them to smack down devils (Acts 12:7). When you know how powerful your side is, you know you have the victory.
"But ye are come unto mount Sion, and unto the city of the living God, the heavenly Jerusalem, and to an innumerable company of angels" Hebrews 12:22
The god of this world (*not the god of this earth*), Satan, has been defeated long ago.
"And having spoiled principalities and powers, he made a shew of them openly, triumphing over them in it" Colossians 2:15
When we command him, instead of speaking about him and what he does, he has to do what we say because the Word, the greater one is in us. The kingdom of heaven is in us.
"Behold, I give unto you power to tread on serpents and scorpions, and over all the power of the enemy: and

nothing shall by any means hurt you. Notwithstanding in this rejoice not, that the spirits are subject unto you; but rather rejoice, because your names are written in heaven." Luke 10:19, 20

When our mouths are speaking the living word of God, angels move on our behalf. Our Lord will confess our name to His angels. His love will cast out the tormenting spirit of fear.

"Also I say to you, whoever confesses Me before men, him the Son of Man also will confess before the angels of God. But he who denies Me before men will be denied before the angels of God" Luke 12:8, 9 (NKJ)

"There is no fear in love; but perfect love casts out fear, because fear involves torment. But he who fears has not been made perfect in love." 1 John 4:18 (NKJ)

Every word out of our mouths can bind or loose devils.

"Death and life are in the power of the tongue..." Proverbs 18:21

"Assuredly, I say to you, whatever you bind on earth will be bound in heaven, and whatever you loose on earth will be loosed in heaven." Matthew 18:18 (NKJ)

Our words will speak life, be idle, murmur or complain or simply be dangerous. We will give account of our words in this life; so even now, we need to let the word flow from us like living water from the Spirit.

"But I say unto you, That every idle word that men shall speak, they shall give account thereof in the day of judgment." Matthew 12:36

When our words are spirit led, they will create life. The way God has set things up on this planet means that we have much power in our mouths. With our angelic help, we don't only have words, but power. They wait on our word. The part of our heavenly contract is to speak. For it is with words of faith that even, "*...things which are seen were not made of things which do appear.*" Hebrews 11:3

"For our gospel came not unto you in word only, but also in power..." 1 Thessalonians 1:5

In the Old Testament days, we seen just two angels involved in fighting.

"...and now will I return to fight with the prince of Persia... and there is none that holdeth with me in these things, but Michael your prince." Daniel 10:20, 21

In the New Testament we sit together with Christ in heavenly places with an innumerable company of angels; "...in heaven their angels do always behold the face of my Father which is in heaven." Matthew 18:10

Sometimes they remind us not to fear, and giving us words of comfort.

"For there stood by me this night an angel of the God to whom I belong and whom I serve, saying, 'Do not be afraid, Paul; you must be brought before Caesar; and indeed God has granted you all those who sail with you.' Therefore take heart, men, for I believe God that it will be just as it was told me." Acts 27:23-25 (NKJ)

Before we were saved, we only thought about us, and *we thought* those thoughts were from us, and not the enemy. The Word gave us a revelation of who we are. We have a higher ranking then the angels. We can step into anything that God has for us. We are never lower than a king or a priest. We can boldly go to the throne of grace for all things pertaining to life and godliness. We can do all things through Christ and have victory in this life, with the angels of the kingdom to help us.

"But ye are a chosen generation, a royal priesthood, an holy nation..." 1 Peter 2:9, 10

"But one in a certain place testified, saying, What is man, that thou art mindful of him? or the son of man, that thou visitest him? Thou madest him a little lower than the angels; thou crownedst him with glory and honour, and didst set him over the works of thy hands: Thou hast put all things in subjection under his feet. For in that he put all in subjection under him, he left nothing that is not put under him. But now we see not yet all things put under him." Hebrews 2:6-8

CHAPTER 14

The Judgment of the Kingdom

A judgment is to make an authoritative decision of separation by an opinion (Greek: aisthesis, akarino, gnome, dikaioma, dike, krima). A righteous judgment (Greek: krisis, dikaiokrisia) is an authoritative decision by God to separating the just, from the unjust. All judgment is committed to the Son, or the Word of God (John 5:22). Because the Word of God has long ago been manifested to destroy the works of the enemy from the foundation of the world (1 John 3:8) and never changes (Heb 13:8), judgment has already been set in motion. The Old Testament is the New Testament *concealed*, the New Testament is the Old Testament *revealed*.

An unchanging law of light that was hidden to most, before the Word was made flesh, was concealed by an enemy, chosen by those who desired to listen to him.

"But if our gospel be hid, it is hid to them that are lost: In whom the god of this world hath blinded the minds of them which believe not, lest the light of the glorious gospel of Christ, who is the image of God, should shine unto them. For we preach not ourselves, but Christ Jesus the Lord; and ourselves your servants for Jesus' sake. For God, who commanded the light to shine out of darkness, hath shined in our hearts, to give the light of the knowledge of the glory of God in the face of Jesus Christ." 2 Corinthians 4:3-6

Though God is no respecter of persons, there are many who are called, few chosen (*sent*) and faithful (Matt 22:14; Rev 17:14), stepping into predestination by *choice*.

"For whom he did foreknow, he also did predestinate to be conformed to the image of his Son, that he might be the firstborn among many brethren. Moreover whom he did predestinate, them he also called: and whom he called, them he also justified..." Romans 8:29, 30

Those who have judged God faithful, and abide in the vine, or live "above the law" in faith, are purged (*or pruned*) to make more fruit, with a residency prepared for them in the house of God (John 15:1-5). There are three wills of God for us; acceptable, good and perfect or: thirty, sixty and a hundredfold. After the former and latter rain, when the fruit is ripe, the Lord will come for His harvest.

"Be patient therefore, brethren, unto the coming of the Lord. Behold, the husbandman waiteth for the precious fruit of the earth, and hath long patience for it, until he receive the early and latter rain." James 5:7

In the bible there is a gathering together in three parts of the harvest of souls. In the Old Testament, which was a shadow of things to come (Col 3:16), there were three parts of the harvest:

The first fruits, or *Bikkurim* the consecrated priest would offer the first ripened grain or fruit and bring it to the holy temple [*see also Ex 13:2*], or in later days, the farmer would tie a reed band or other distinguishing mark to the temple and declare, "These are the first fruits" which would bless the rest of the harvest. The main harvest; The majority of the grain or grapes would be gathered for the people. (Lev 19:9) The gleaning; the corners of the field, the remnant, would be for the poor and the widows (Lev 19:10).

All males, 20 and up, were required to go to three of the feasts (Passover, Pentecost, Feast of tabernacles) at the sound of the trumpet (Ex 23:17, Num 10:4)

In the New Testament, the first fruits of the church are harvested out the field (the world) to the temple in heaven, before the tribulation (*which some call 'rapture' from Jerome's Latin translation; repere*)

"But every man in his own order: Christ the firstfruits; afterward they that are Christ's at his coming." 1 Corinthians 15:23

"For the Lord himself shall descend from heaven with a shout, with the voice of the archangel, and with the trump of God: and the dead in Christ shall rise first: Then we which are alive and remain shall be caught up together with them in the clouds, to meet the Lord in the air: and so shall we ever be with the Lord." 1 Thessalonians 4:16, 17

The main harvest: In the middle of the 'tribulation' period an angel thrust in his sickle to reap.

"And another angel came out of the temple, crying with a loud voice to Him who sat on the cloud, 'Thrust in Your sickle and reap, for the time has come for You to reap, for the harvest of the earth is ripe." Revelation 14:15 (NKJ)

The gleaning; and then the second coming, after heaven says "*Come out of her my people*" (Rev 18:4) for all who are sealed unto the day of redemption (Eph 4:30).

"Then another angel came out of the temple which is in heaven, he also having a sharp sickle. And another angel came out from the altar, who had power over fire, and he cried with a loud cry to him who had the sharp sickle, saying, 'Thrust in your sharp sickle and gather the clusters of the vine of the earth, for her grapes are fully ripe" Revelation 14:18 (KNJ)

"Having made known unto us the mystery of his will, according to his good pleasure which he hath purposed in himself: That in the dispensation of the fulness of times he might gather together in one all things in Christ, both which are in heaven, and which are on earth; even in him" Ephesians 1:9,10

"So shall it be at the end of the world: the angels shall come forth, and sever the wicked from among the just" Matthew 13:49

In the Old Testament times, there were three harvests that the feasts were centered around.

The barley harvest (barley is winnowed with a big fork, tossed in the air, with the chaff easily taken separated by the wind), the wheat harvest (wheat is harder to take away the wheat from the chaff. This was usually done with a "tribulon" (Latin) or a hard board with glass and/or metal, sometimes pulled by animals), and the grape harvest, (the flesh of the grapes were crushed, to be harvested).

In the New Testament, Jesus made a distinction between servants and friends.

"You are My friends if you do whatever I command you. No longer do I call you servants, for a servant does not know what his master is doing; but I have called you friends, for all things that I heard from My Father I have made known to you." John 15:14, 15 (NKJ)

"Wherefore thou art no more a servant, but a son; and if a son, then an heir of God through Christ." Galatians 4:7

Generally, the gospels were written for the unsaved, the epistles for the saved, and the book of Revelation for servants (Rev 1:1). As we've seen in the parables of talents and virgins, some foolish and lazy servants received **judgment** to a prison of outer darkness.

"For the time is come that judgment must begin at the house of God: and if it first begin at us, what shall the end be of them that obey not the gospel of God?" 1 Peter 4:17

We've also seen another servant cast into prison *until* he paid his debt for the wages of sinfulness.

"And his fellowservant fell down at his feet, and besought him, saying, Have patience with me, and I will pay thee all. And he would not: but went and cast him into prison, till he should pay the debt." Matthew 18:29, 30

Some covenant servants will delay their entrance into the promised land of rest by their decisions. The servants who have the seal of God will have a limited amount of protection in the prison of tribulation. The servants who knew better, but chose to be disobedient, will be responsible for what they have been given.

"And that servant, which knew his lord's will, and prepared not himself, neither did according to his will, shall be beaten with many stripes. But he that knew not, and did commit things worthy of stripes, shall be beaten with few stripes. For unto whomsoever much is given, of him shall be much required: and to whom men have committed much, of him they will ask the more." Luke 12:47, 48

There are those who are holy, and those who are righteous, and some unjust (Rev 22:11). In the tribulation period, two 3 1/2 year periods, the wrath of the Lamb (Rev 6:16, Rev 7:14) and the wrath of God (Rev 14:19) will continue trials of faith. Many will follow delusions, seeking for life, but finding none.

"And for this cause God shall send them strong delusion, that they should believe a lie" 2 Thessalonians 2:11

"And he doeth great wonders, so that he maketh fire come down from heaven on the earth in the sight of men, and deceiveth them that dwell on the earth by the means of those miracles which he had power to do in the sight of the beast; saying to them that dwell on the earth, that they should make an image to the beast, which had the wound by a sword, and did live." Revelation 13:13, 14

Many saints who remain will not accept the mark or number of the beast (Rev 13:7-8, 16). Many Jews who are looking for the Messiah will find Jesus.

"And one shall say unto him, What are these wounds in thine hands? Then he shall answer, Those with which I was wounded in the house of my friends." Zechariah 13:6

"And I saw another angel...Saying, Hurt not the earth, neither the sea, nor the trees, till we have sealed the servants of our God in their foreheads. And I heard the number of them which were sealed: and there were sealed an hundred and forty and four thousand of all the tribes of the children of Israel." Revelation 7:3, 4

We should all *"contend for the faith that was once delivered to the saints"* (Jude 3). We will all sit at the judgment seat.

"For we must all appear before the judgment seat of Christ; that every one may receive the things done in his body, according to that he hath done, whether it be good or bad." 2 Corinthians 5:10

Before the end, we will also stand on the side of judgment.

"Do ye not know that the saints shall judge the world? and if the world shall be judged by you, are ye unworthy to judge the smallest matters? Know ye not that we shall judge angels? ..." 1 Corinthians 6:2, 3

"The men of Nineveh shall rise in judgment with this generation, and shall condemn it: because they repented at the preaching of Jonas; and, behold, a greater than Jonas is here. The queen of the south shall rise up in the judgment with this generation, and shall condemn it: for she came from the uttermost parts of the earth to hear the wisdom of Solomon; and, behold, a greater than Solomon is here." Matthew 12:41, 42

CHAPTER 15

The Changing of the Kingdom

In many countries, people have accepted Islam, Hinduism and others, because of the "Christians" that didn't take their own bible as a way of life. Many Christian converts never grow up, being poorly nourished from compromising or ignorant leadership. With many churches in division over gifts of the Spirit, gay leadership, traditions, etc., the kingdom divided against itself turns away seekers who, in this country receive around 70% of their information about God from the media and perhaps 2% from enlightened church goers that are friends, classmates or co-workers. The devil knew that if he could speak through the leader at a church, he could (*temporarily*) claim many territories. Although he knows he only has a short time, his mission is to delay or pause God's plan in us individually and corporately, to buy himself more time.

Through misdirection the adversary stole away time, place and presence. For many years, the kingdom became an idea only for the future (i.e. heaven or "pie in the sky"), it did not show the available power for the present life that we live here on earth. When the kingdom appeared to be a *faraway* place, it took away the fellowship and availability of sitting together in heavenly places with the Lord. When the connection to God was limited to a shout, dance or an entertaining "motivational speaker", without the fruits of repentance, the presence of God was limited for some to church attendance (*instead of lifestyle*) for a small (*or large*) donation. Many messages had enough milk to keep us hanging on, but in the pivotal time we are living in now, we need to step up to a higher level. Some places were basically *only* evangelical in nature where you just heard the message of being born again, but not a lot about being truly discipled. Other places consistently dealt with sin issues for decades without much change.

Many places that evangelists are not sent out, benchwarmers become the norm and outreach is a marquee or a line in the yellow pages. In other recent statistics, 98% of all professed Christians have never led anyone to Christ. 89% of us have never given out a tract. Hal Rahman states that in 1995 with 3.3 trillion dollars in total church treasuries, 80% of this was for 'inside the walls'. 1.7% went to outreach and missions. In 2005, out of over 5 trillion dollars, 0.7% went to outreach. Countries throughout the world fare differently. In Northern Europe, there are over $2,000,000 spent per new baptized member. The U.S. is close to that at $1,551,466. Mozambique's at $1,366. A change is coming.

In the early church's fivefold ministries, there was outside help from apostles, prophets and evangelists who were part of one body without separate manmade denominations. Even though the New Testament refers to the *"pastor"* one time, many churches attempt to function with only this one (*although necessary*) gift. Though many of these started out with the fire; organization, individualism, division, pride and humanism put these fires out. The burdens put on an individual pastor would increase the tightrope that he walked upon. In recent U.S. findings, 45% of pastors suffer from burnout, 70% say they have no friends, 80% say their job is negatively affecting their family, 90% claim they were not trained to handle their occupation, 95% struggle with discouragement and 37% say they are currently struggling with internet porn or some are involved with extra-marital relationships. When there is a hope in every man's spirit to find the kingdom (righteousness, peace and joy in the Holy Ghost), some leaders unintentionally stunt growth or weaken under the pressure of pleasing people or finances (*like they were supposed to build the church instead of Jesus*). A leader should be able to train Christian soldiers like a drill sergeant, and make disciples instead of dependents. Times are changing.

In the positions of the fivefold ministries (*Apostles, Prophets, Evangelist, Pastors, Teachers*) part of our job description is for the perfecting of the saints, so they can be perfect, or arrive to a spiritual maturity as our Father in heaven is. The fruit you produce is evident to your calling.

"And he gave some, apostles; and some, prophets; and some, evangelists; and some, pastors and teachers; For the perfecting of the saints, for the work of the ministry, for the edifying of the body of Christ: till we all come in the unity of the faith, and of the knowledge of the Son of God, unto a perfect man, unto the measure of the stature of the fulness of Christ" Ephesians 4:11-13

"Be ye therefore perfect, even as your Father which is in heaven is perfect." Matthew 5:48

To perfect anything that is lacking in their faith.

"Whom we preach, warning every man, and teaching every man in all wisdom; that we may present every man perfect in Christ Jesus" Colossians 1:28

"Night and day praying exceedingly that we might see your face, and might perfect that which is lacking in your faith?" 1 Thessalonians 3:10

When we have this not only as a goal, but an expectation of answered prayer, the grace of God and sacrificial work, the spirit to spirit encouragement will exponentially multiply interest, miracles, signs and wonders, bringing back the days of hundreds and thousands being saved and filled in the same service at a time. Our 'spiritual children' are to have more than us, providing fruitful proof of our spiritual legacy and anointing. Our pastors are not to be burned out, but on fire.

People look upon us who are supernatural (*because His spirit is upon ALL flesh*) with their spirit, knowing that there is something in us that can deliver them from any lack, disease, worry or fear. Our *disciples* can only go as far as we take them. We must keep our *spiritual batteries* charged to deliver the immediacies of God to our flocks, raise the level of expectation to consistency, and put away every sin from our lives.

"Wherefore seeing we also are compassed about with so great a cloud of witnesses, let us lay aside every weight, and the sin which doth so easily beset us..." Hebrews 12:1

Even simple delegation of work can help, Jesus had only twelve, but with great results. Moses delayed the delegation (*suggested by Jethro*) to allow the elders of Israel to judge the matters of the people with unfruitful results. With spiritual wickedness in high places and every high thing that exalts itself against God already in place; we cannot afford to be our own enemy. A kingdom divided against itself cannot stand. When our submission is complete, it brings the permanencies of a God in us that shall not be moved or shaken, and brings the awareness to others that there is a place in God for them.

Our natural resistance to God falls when we see purpose. When we perceive that God has chosen us to do His will, we will also perceive the Holy Spirit will back us up through our prayers, intercession, and involvement. The revelation of God comes when we submit to, and have confidence in His way of thinking. This agreement has resulted in the fact that there are now more people being saved and equipped than at any other time in history. More Muslims have turned to Christ in the last 10 years than the last previous 1,000. In India, the Mizoram state is now 87% Christian and the Nagaland state has 'gone with the Wind' with over 90%. Many people in third world countries never had the "conditioning" of religion or of mixing world conformity with the Message during their lives, will press into the kingdom quicker and more effectively. The Southern hemisphere is already experiencing greater miracles and growth compared to their Northern counterparts. Signs and wonders of many other nations will encourage the U.S. for the most exciting revival ever for the end time generation. We will see God's will being done in services where all are filled and healed. The knowledge of the Lord will cover the earth from sea to sea. No matter what temporary circumstances we see, The **Kingdom** is changing for the better.

"For this cause we also, since the day we heard it, do not cease to pray for you, and to desire that ye might be filled with the knowledge of his will in all wisdom and spiritual understanding.." Colossians 1:9

CHAPTER 16

The Near Future of the Kingdom

The time is coming when the world will have a great respect for the church. Even now the spiritual "tug of war" is becoming easier with over 20 million soldiers per year putting their hands to the plow. Many of these prayer warriors are in spiritual intercession for the lost and non-discipled. We are coming to a place where miracles multiply rapidly and exponentially, not unlike the industrial and computer revolution in the U.S. The last few years before the body of Christ meets the Lord in the air, will see an unprecedented display of signs, wonders and power. They will be seen on popular television, as the proof of the living Word will win over many souls. People will not ask the Lord when He is going to show up, but watch Him as He shows Himself mightily among His children. The bashful will become the brave, the tale-bearer will tell of God, the drug-distributor will become the tract-distributor, the one who creeps in the shadows will heal with his shadow, the one who flashed gang signs we be showing signs and wonders, and the murderer will lose his influence because his victims will be raised from the dead.

Many people that have been searching for God will jump on the "bandwagon" of faith and glorify God. People will not deceive themselves by being a hearer and not a doer. Prayers will be back in schools with even young children healing and ejecting demons. Abortion clinics will be shut down. Our judges will consult the Spirit for decisions. Poor people will be hard to find. Born again diseased people will become history as power replaces pity and the super natural negates sympathy. The asthma spirit will be on the run, backed up into a small corner on the planet. When the body of Christ comes into the unity and power that it is accurately called to, when the saints of God are about to be presented without spot or wrinkle as prophesied, people will not ask where is God, but will run to Him or from Him.

"That he might present it to himself a glorious church, not having spot, or wrinkle, or any such thing; but that it should be holy and without blemish." Ephesians 5:27

God awaits the presentation of the bride (the body of Christ) who has been prepared by the Holy Spirit.

"…the marriage of the Lamb has come, and his wife has made herself ready." Revelation 19:7 (NKJ)

This won't be a weak, wimpy bride that can't come into agreement cross-denominationally, or fight with each other like little brothers, but one with one accord with the Head of the church and as a body. The rapture will not "brain wash" us, but the blood that will cleanse us thoroughly from all unrighteousness while we are on the planet. In the last days of the end time generation, some will get raised from the dead, taught the Word and renew their mind. A kingdom that is not divided against itself will stand against any wiles of the devil. As Jesus spoiled principalities and powers and made a show of them openly in the spiritual world (Colossians 2:15), we will make a show of the enemy openly in the natural. The whole armour of God will continuously stay on us, unless we take off the belt of truth to whip the devil with it!

The corperate anointing will help the last of the struggling churches to connect with God. The strong will easily ignite the weak. Some will look at dysfunctional churches and say "What's wrong with that church? Why did they let that person die? Why don't they raise him from the dead?" "Why do they let that person who was lame from his mother's womb come to church every Sunday begging, instead of healing them?" "Why didn't they calm that storm? Doesn't everyone know how to flow with the anointing?"

At that time when just about every enemy is defeated, all the body will have left to say is come, Lord Jesus. As the demons run away in terror Satan will be begging for a rapture to come. The angels of God will have to literally pull some of us off fighting devils when it happens. Heaven will have another announcement for him: **"And the seventh angel sounded; and there were great voices in heaven, saying, The kingdoms of this world are become the kingdoms of our Lord, and of his Christ; and he shall reign for ever and ever." Revelation 11:15**

Get ready for the very near future coming of the kingdom.

CHAPTER 17

The Millennium of the Kingdom

God is preparing us for an eternity where all will be like Him in likeness and spirit. We are training for reigning. In his Word, He has given us insight, to what He wants us to know about things to come (John 16:13). Without a vision the people perish (Proverbs 29:18). With a vision and view of the finish line, the fire of adrenaline kicks in for a mighty finish. Without the view blinding devil to deceive, the vision will become clearer.

"And I saw an angel come down from heaven, having the key of the bottomless pit and a great chain in his hand. And he laid hold on the dragon, that old serpent, which is the Devil, and Satan, and bound him a thousand years, and cast him into the bottomless pit, and shut him up, and set a seal upon him, that he should deceive the nations no more, till the thousand years should be fulfilled: and after that he must be loosed a little season." Revelation 20:1-3

When the second coming of the Lord happens or when He comes all the way down to the Earth (*not just the air*), His family who will have a physical change, will still need to be taught of God.

"...when he shall appear, we shall be like Him; for we shall see him as he is" (1 John 3:2)

We will have a great awareness of people places and things as the rich man did when seeing Abraham and Lazarus (Luke 16:23), or when Paul prophesied he would see face to face and; "Then shall I know even as also I am known" (1 Corinthians 13:12). We will have years of discovery in a relationship with the Word, living without the enemy, and removing the enemy of self. There will still be a need to renew our mind. The need to remove deep seed planted unclean thoughts (*like fantasies of the opposite sex, selfish attention seeking behavior or other thoughts that are not kingdom ways of thinking*). There will still be a need to eliminate humanistic comparisons of each other. We've seen in Jesus' examples of the kingdom regarding what is lawful and just to God, compared to men.

"But when the first came, they supposed that they would receive more; and they likewise received each a denarius. And when they had received *it,* they complained against the landowner, saying, 'These last *men* have worked *only* one hour, and you made them equal to us who have borne the burden and the heat of the day.' But he answered one of them and said, 'Friend, I am doing you no wrong. Did you not agree with me for a denarius? Take *what is* yours and go your way. I wish to give to this last man *the same* as to you. Is it not lawful for me to do what I wish with my own things? Or is your eye evil because I am good?" Matthew 20:10-15 (NKJ)

"And he said to those who stood by, 'Take the mina from him, and give *it* to him who has ten minas.' (But they said to him, 'Master, he has ten minas.') 'For I say to you, that to everyone who has will be given; and from him who does not have, even what he has will be taken away from him." Luke 19:24-26 (NKJ)

The knowledge of the Lord will be available and cover the earth from sea to sea. At this time, there is no "magic wand" to make us think just like God, but we will receive teaching of the Spirit of God, and our minds will be open without distraction from the enemy on the outside of us. When God shows us our own nature, we will only need to work on the "enemy within". Even all who died young, and the newly birthed Christians and Jews will make decisions to obey the love of God, or be rebels like Lucifer, who was in the presence of God and the Holy angels, but decided to go on his own. There has never been any respecter of person with God (Acts 10:34). All will have the chance to accept or reject God. Children resting in peace will have a more conducive atmosphere (2 Samuel 2:23) of His acceptance, but the trial of our faith on earth is much more precious than gold, being found unto praise and honor and glory at the appearing of Jesus Christ (1 Peter 1:5-9). Our "commander in chief" will have led us to a great victory over a most formidable enemy.

After the first fruits of Christ sit together with past generation saints, and all the marriage guests from the highways and hedges have been compelled to come, the seven year temporary tribulation period of outer darkness (see Matthew 18:30, Revelation 18:4), (*the place away from the presence of the Spirit of God is*) will be over. God's servants, friends (Matthew 22:12, 13) and children of the kingdom will be in the presence of the Lord.

"And I say unto you, That many shall come from the east and west, and shall sit down with Abraham, and Isaac, and Jacob, in the kingdom of heaven. But the children of the kingdom shall be cast out into outer darkness..." Matthew 8:11, 12

The saints that are Christ's after His coming will meet the first fruits of Christ.

● "But now is Christ risen from the dead, and become the firstfruits of them that slept. For since by man came death, by man came also the resurrection of the dead. For as in Adam all die, even so in Christ shall all be made alive. But every man in his own order: Christ the firstfruits; afterward they that are Christ's at his coming." 1 Corinthians 15:20-23

And the royal priesthood will reign as kings on thrones and judge men and angels (1 Corinthians 6:2, 3, Matthew 12:41, 42).

"And I saw thrones, and they sat upon them, and judgment was given unto them: and I saw the souls of them that were beheaded for the witness of Jesus, and for the word of God, and which had not worshipped the beast, neither his image, neither had received his mark upon their foreheads, or in their hands; and they lived and reigned with Christ a thousand years. But the rest of the dead lived not again until the thousand years were finished. This is the first resurrection. Blessed and holy is he that hath part in the first resurrection: on such the second death hath no power, but they shall be priests of God and of Christ, and shall reign with him a thousand years." Revelation 20:4-6

In the millennium period, the Word of God, thoroughly filled within the body of Christ, continues to replenish the earth. In Isaiah 65:17 where it is written *"I will create a new heaven and earth"* is an old idiom meaning; *"I will create a new world order with true justice and peace"*. This is a time where all the final layers of justice will be served. Ever since Lucifer, there has always been a place away from God's way of Life. If anybody has tasted of the heavenly gift, and were made partakers of the Holy Ghost falls away, it would be impossible to renew them to repentance (see Hebrews 6:4-6). In time, all old worldly kinds of injustices will be forgotten. It will be a time of abundance, great laughter, joy and no lack for all. The Old Testament prophets described pieces of the millennium period of peace, before death and hell (Revelation 20:15) are thrown into the lake of fire.

"And it shall come to pass in the last days, that the mountain of the LORD's house shall be established in the top of the mountains, and shall be exalted above the hills; and all nations shall flow unto it. And many people shall go and say, Come ye, and let us go up to the mountain of the LORD, to the house of the God of Jacob; and he will teach us of his ways, and we will walk in his paths: for out of Zion shall go forth the law, and the word of the LORD from Jerusalem. And he shall judge among the nations, and shall rebuke many people: and they shall beat their swords into plowshares, and their spears into pruninghooks: nation shall not lift up sword against nation, neither shall they learn war any more." Isaiah 2:2-4

"And I will rejoice in Jerusalem, and joy in my people: and the voice of weeping shall be no more heard in her, nor the voice of crying. There shall be no more thence an infant of days, nor an old man that hath not filled his days: for the child shall die an hundred years old; but the sinner being an hundred years old shall be accursed. And they shall build houses, and inhabit them; and they shall plant vineyards, and eat the fruit of them. They shall not build, and another inhabit; they shall not plant, and another eat: for as the days of a tree are the days of my people, and mine elect shall long enjoy the work of their hands. They shall not labour in vain, nor bring forth for trouble; for they are the seed of the blessed of the LORD, and their offspring with them. And it shall come to pass, that before they call, I will answer; and while they are yet speaking, I will hear. The wolf and the lamb shall feed together, and the lion shall eat straw like the bullock: and dust shall be the serpent's meat. They shall not hurt

**nor destroy in all my holy mountain, saith the LORD."
Isaiah 65:19-25**

In those days, there will be no more dying babies. The only dying there will be sinners who leave that spiritual estate and are cut off (accursed) like the fallen angels. Every one shall fulfill their days. Being only 100 will be dying young, just as it would have been in the days before Noah when Adam lived to be 930 years old, and his son Seth lived to be 912 (Gen 5:5,8). And in this time, all who have forsaken houses, family or lands, will receive a hundredfold (Mark 10:29, 30). And, in the world to come, their works will follow them. In the 25th verse we see the idiom *"The wolf and the lamb feed together,"*, meaning, *"A dictatorship and a meek nation trading and living together in peace."* We also the idiom *"Dust shall be the serpent's meat,"* meaning, *"The oppressor shall be reduced to poverty."* Nations will bring their honor to it, as the windows in heaven will always be open. Zechariah continues:

"And the LORD shall be king over all the earth: in that day shall there be one LORD, and his name one. All the land shall be turned as a plain from Geba to Rimmon south of Jerusalem: and it shall be lifted up, and inhabited in her place, from Benjamin's gate unto the place of the first gate, unto the corner gate, and from the tower of Hananeel unto the king's winepresses. And men shall dwell in it, and there shall be no more utter destruction; but Jerusalem shall be safely inhabited." Zechariah 14:9-11

"Behold, the days come, saith the LORD, that I will make a new covenant with the house of Israel, and with the house of Judah...I put my law in their inward parts, and write it in their hearts; and will be their God, and they shall be my people. And they shall teach no more every man his neighbour, and every man his brother, saying, Know the LORD: for they shall all know me, from the

least of them unto the greatest of them, saith the LORD: for I will forgive their iniquity, and I will remember their sin no more." Jeremiah 31:31-34

The teaching will take time and there will be an abundance of it. We will be able to return to the knowledge of the now "unknown tongue," our built-in language (Adam didn't have to learn a language) which was spoken through the first eleven chapters of Genesis when, "*the whole earth was of one language and one speech*" (Genesis 11:1). The LORD said: **"For I will turn to the people a pure language, that they may all call upon the name of the LORD, to serve him with one consent." Zephaniah 3:9** Or, as Paul said in 1 Corinthians 13:1; "*Though I speak with the tongues of men and angels...*"

When Satan is loosed for a season, and goes seeking those who he may devour, the earthly rebels will be gathered together for one last fight against the city of God.

"And when the thousand years are expired, Satan shall be loosed out of his prison, And shall go out to deceive the nations which are in the four quarters of the earth, Gog and Magog, to gather them together to battle: the number of whom is as the sand of the sea. And they went up on the breadth of the earth, and compassed the camp of the saints about, and the beloved city: and fire came down from God out of heaven, and devoured them." Revelation 20:7-9

God will take the vengeance that belongs to Him with the presence of the Lord.

"Seeing it is a righteous thing with God to recompense tribulation to them that trouble you; and to you who are troubled rest with us, when the Lord Jesus shall be revealed from heaven with his mighty angels, in flaming fire taking vengeance on them that know not God, and that obey not the gospel of our Lord Jesus Christ: Who shall be punished with everlasting destruction from the

presence of the Lord, and from the glory of his power; <u>When he shall come to be glorified in his saints</u>, and to be admired in all them that believe (because our testimony among you was believed) in that day." 2 Thessalonians 1:6-10

When the end of the millennium period comes, death, the last enemy is destroyed,

"Then cometh the end, when he shall have delivered up the kingdom to God, even the Father; when he shall have put down all rule and all authority and power. For he must reign, till he hath put all enemies under his feet. The last enemy that shall be destroyed is death." 1 Corinthians 15:24-26

"And the kingdom and dominion, and the greatness of the kingdom under the whole heaven, shall be given to the people of the saints of the most High, whose kingdom is an everlasting kingdom, and all dominions shall serve and obey him. Hitherto (now) is the end of the matter..." Daniel 7:27, 28

And at the very last trump, when the kingdom is delivered, and there is no place found for the heaven and earth (Revelation 20:11), and death is swallowed up in victory, we will all be changed.

"Behold, I shew you a mystery; We shall not all sleep, but we shall all be changed, in a moment, in the twinkling of an eye, at the last trump: for the trumpet shall sound, and the dead shall be raised incorruptible, and we shall be changed." 1 Corinthians 15:51, 52

"And many of them that sleep in the dust of the earth shall awake, some to everlasting life, and some to shame and everlasting contempt. And they that be wise shall shine as the brightness of the firmament; and they that turn many to righteousness as the stars for ever and ever." Daniel 12:2, 3

God's plan has always been for men to replenish the earth through us, who He has given the command, authority and jurisdiction to. His plans will come to pass before heaven and earth passes away.

"**For I know the thoughts that I think toward you, saith the LORD, thoughts of peace, and not of evil, to give you an expected end.**" Jeremiah 29:11

CHAPTER 18

Your Place in the Kingdom

Through the blood of Jesus and the power of the Holy Spirit, you have been granted access in the Kingdom of God. Your life is constantly ready for change, to change the world. This is the change that prophecy has always spoken about throughout the bible, to prepare a place for you in the kingdom. The power and presence that seems so foreign and unreal to many, or too good to be true, has been seen for centuries in the black and white pages of the bible, and has finally been revealed to you as a son of the King. You are ready for a greater level. You have moved from the devils house of worry, fear, doubt and the "what about me?" attitude, to God's untouchable house of perfect peace, asking "What about Him?"

"You will keep *him* in perfect peace, *Whose* mind *is* stayed *on You,* Because he trusts in You." Isaiah 26:3 (NKJ)

When you have a promise from God's Word, you never have to fear.

"For God hath not given us the spirit of fear; but of power, and of love, and of a sound mind." 2 Timothy 1:7

The "old man" is outdated and useless to you, and cannot understand where you're going.

"But the natural man receiveth not the things of the Spirit of God: for they are foolishness unto him: neither can he know them, because they are spiritually discerned." 1 Corinthians 2:14

"...be renewed in the spirit of your mind; and that ye put on the new man, which after God is created in righteousness and true holiness." Ephesians 4:24, 25

Your hunger for the living Word of God has let you know that you're not waiting on a *move of God*, but God's waiting for a move from you, for you to put on the new man; because He's not going to do it for you. You are no longer a dependent, but a disciple. You are no longer a servant, but a friend.

"No longer do I call you servants, for a servant does not know what his master is doing; but I have called you friends, for all things that I heard from My Father I have made known to you" John 15:15 (NKJ)

You have direct access to God. Jesus never said, *"This is for me, but not for you,"* but He said we will do even greater things.

"Verily, verily, I say unto you, He that believeth on me, the works that I do shall he do also; and greater works than these shall he do; because I go unto my Father." John 14:12

You will have whatever you have faith to have.

"Therefore I say to you, whatever things you ask when you pray, believe that you receive *them,* and you will have *them*." Mark 11:24 (NKJ)

When His disciples asked Him about the stormy sea, He said *"Where is your faith?"* or when feeding the 5,000 – *"You feed them."* He wouldn't tell us to do it without knowing that the power is already available, even though He did comment about His disciples having little faith. Once we have a Word on a situation, our faith will grow when we meditate on it. Once we gain greater confidence in His Word, people will discern the anointing upon us and know we can intercede for them. The angelic power is available to back up the words of faith from our mouth.

You will come into agreement to what you don't see, but *know*. When you "tune in" to the frequency of the Holy Spirit, you are ready for God to show you the path of abundant life.

"In all your ways acknowledge him, and he shall direct your paths." Proverbs 3:6 (NKJ)

The prophets of the Old Testament, and John, talked about a day to come. Jesus started speaking the word by saying, "*This day*," is this scripture fulfilled. From the time Jesus walked on the earth, the day that was coming became the day that is. Even now the long awaited reality of God residing in His people is being fulfilled.

"Jesus answered and said unto him, If a man love me, he will keep my words: and my Father will love him, and we will come unto him, and make our abode with him." John 14:23

Now that Jesus has come to give you power, the "was," or the "old man" in your life, is being crucified; acceleration is the way of getting things done, and the mind of Jesus has opened a realm in heavenly places for your abundance.

"... give diligence to make your calling and election sure: for if ye do these things, ye shall never fall: For so an entrance shall be ministered unto you abundantly into the everlasting kingdom of our Lord and Saviour Jesus Christ." 2 Peter 1:10, 11

After the order of Melchisedec and the priesthood of Jesus, you are part of a royal priesthood, to have dominion over the planet, representing the Father, by the guidance and power of his Holy Spirit, and influence others with your confidence in God's will.

"But you *are* a chosen generation, a royal priesthood, a holy nation, His own special people, that you may

proclaim the praises of Him who called you out of darkness into His marvelous light" 1 Peter 2:9 (NKJ)

In the beginning was the Word, Who created all things, framing the worlds.

"Through faith we understand that the worlds were framed by the word of God, so that things which are seen were not made of things which do appear." Hebrews 11:3

"Who (Jesus) is the image of the invisible God, the firstborn of every creature: For by him were all things created, that are in heaven, and that are in earth, visible and invisible, whether they be thrones, or dominions, or principalities, or powers: all things were created by him, and for him" Colossians 1:15, 16

And now, you have the same Word *and* the Spirit of God to do great things, which is more than enough power. God will not show you a place where He won't take you. Your decisions are vital and will contribute to the body of Christ. It is time to prepare for a testimony; to literally speak into your life things you've never had and power you've never experienced. Your words will dictate your life and the atmosphere around you because *"Death and life are in the power of the tongue"* (Proverbs 18:21)

He has for you an impartation of permanency, so that the immediacies of God will keep happening in your life. Your confidence and anointing will influence the lives of many others. Your trust in Him keeps your high rank in the kingdom.

"Therefore do not cast away your confidence, which has great reward" Hebrews 10:35 (NKJ)

In His rest, there is no hesitation, no waiting; just the expectancy of manifestations from a living Jesus that doesn't just rest in peace, but *rules in peace*. Have faith in God.

You are justified (just as if you've never sinned) by our ever-interceding Jesus, who intercedes within us; always available to represent us to our Father.

"Who is he that condemneth? It is Christ that died, yea rather, that is risen again, who is even at the right hand of God, who also maketh intercession for us." Romans 8:34

"Wherefore he is able also to save them to the uttermost that come unto God by him, seeing he ever liveth to make intercession for them." Hebrews 7:25

In God's presence, you *are* perfect in the kingdom, being made blameless by the Son.

"Be ye therefore perfect, even as your Father which is in heaven is perfect." Matthew 5:48

God doesn't see Jesus and you, He sees Jesus *in* you. When we pray in the spirit, there is no difference between you and Jesus, *"because as He is, so are we in this world."* (1 John 4:17)

He always hears you and He always answers yes to your prayers.

"For all the promises of God in him are yea, and in him Amen, unto the glory of God by us." 2 Corinthians 1:20

In your position, you will know that sometimes, evil spirits (*or illegal aliens*) have to be reminded of their place under your feet. We have to also be a revelation to them that Jesus is in us with consistency. Since they even lie to themselves, they will check to see if you're wavering.

"But let him ask in faith, nothing wavering. For he that wavereth is like a wave of the sea driven with the wind and tossed. For let not that man think that he shall receive any thing of the Lord." James 1:6, 7

When you have prayed and gave a death sentence to your "condition," or another person's, they may try to *appeal* their case to you, but you must keep stirring up the gift, staying connected to God's word, having done all to stand, earning great respect in the seen and the unseen world. With God in you, you are *"above the law"* spiritually, and naturally if necessary, with the anointing to make right, the things that are wrong. Miracles are just a manifestation of a higher law. The blood of Jesus paid the price for all deteriorating conditions from the time Adam had sold us into slavery. Keep the change.

Faith is patient. Faith is a substance. Faith is the assurance of the outcome in advance. Faith doesn't talk about the power, it delivers it.

"For the kingdom of God is not in word, but in power." 1 Corinthians 4:20

"For our gospel came not unto you in word only, but also in power, and in the Holy Ghost, and in much assurance..." 1 Thessalonians 1:5

Faith takes the Word of God at face value, knowing that God doesn't lie or change. Have faith in God. You will not judge his word as another opinion, or a possibility, but a promise of performance in your life to do exceedingly more than you can ask or think. Since your thoughts and prayers are inspired from heaven in the first place, you can feel his nudge on your inner man to perform the desires of His heart, as they become the desire of yours.

You have judged Him faithful to fulfill all things, knowing that there is no isolated incident that the blood of Jesus will not cover to heal. Knowing that Jesus never said He will heal the next day or much later, but always in the present time. When you have a now anointing, your authority is relevant to now power. When miracles and holy living seem like such a small and natural thing to do, your confidence will reflect on those who are in the world and bring them out of darkness. There are many people waiting for someone like you with the revelation of power you have. Some will start off as an "average" church member like Stephan, who had great faith with miracles following. Signs and wonders become normal as you set your affections on things above.

"If ye then be risen with Christ, seek those things which are above, where Christ sitteth on the right hand of God. Set your affection on things above, not on things on the earth." Colossians 3:1, 2

Rejoice. God has given you a name written in heaven that describes exactly who *you* are in the kingdom, according to the decisions you will make in your life. Many will be called to a higher office of a prophet, apostle, pastor or evangelist. Your separation from the things of the world will place you in the position of intercession and kingdom building with a generation that will not be buried, but will fly away when all is fulfilled. Welcome. This is your place in the kingdom of God.

Bibliography

Lamsa, George *Idioms in the Bible explained and Key to the Original Gospels.* New York, NY: HarperCollins Publishers 1931, 1971, 1985

The Temple Institute. *The Festival of Shavout: Bringing the Firstfruits to the Temple* (English). Jerusalem 2007

Lighthouse Chapel, *World Watch* Bellflower CA

Wikipedia, 2007

Rahman, Hal, quoted at *Azusa Street Centennial*, 2006

Barret, David and Johnson, Todd *World Christian Trends* Pasadena, CA 2004

Strong, James The *New Strongs Exhaustive Concordance of the Bible* Thomas Nelson Publishers Nashville TN 1984

Contact info: jdaniellowe@yahoo.com

Printed in the United States
205521BV00001B/20/P